THE HISTORY OF Haute Couture 1850-1950

THE HISTORY OF HISTORY OF Haute Couture 1850– 1950

Diana de Marly

HOLMES & MEIER PUBLISHERS, INC.
New York

The author is most grateful to the following for their assistance:

To H.R.H. Princess Alice, Countess of Athlone; to the late Earl Mountbatten of Burma; to the Hon. Lady Lindsay, formerly Duchess of Westminster; and to Mrs Elizabeth Collins MBE, secretary to the late Lady Mountbatten, for their memories of patronising couture houses.

To Hardy Amies CVO, to Monsieur Roger Worth and Monsieur Maurice Worth for their thoughts on working as couturiers.

To the staff of the following collections and libraries: Penny Byrde of the Costume Research Centre, Bath; to the British Library and the Colindale Newspaper Library; to the National Art Library at the Victoria and Albert Museum; to the National Library of Economics and Political Science; the Newport Library of the Isle of Wight; and to Westminster City Libraries. Ms Jane Bridgeman kindly placed her modern files at my disposal.

All translations in the text are by the author.

1 *Frontispiece* The founding father of
Parisian haute couture, Charles
Frederick Worth, 1825–95. Engraving
by F. Méaule after photograph by
Felix Nadar.

First published in the United States of America 1980 by
Holmes & Meier Publishers, Inc.
30 Irving Place
New York, N.Y. 10003

Copyright © 1980 by Diana de Marly

Library of Congress Cataloging in Publication Data
De Marly, Diana.
    The history of haute couture, 1850–1950.

    Bibliography: p.
    Includes index.
    1. Fashion – History – 19th century.
2. Fashion – History – 20th century.   I. Title.
TT504.D45   391'.07'2   79-22987

ISBN 0-8419-0586-X

Printed in Great Britain

Contents

List of Illustrations

23 Callot Soeurs afternoon gown. *Les Modes*, Dec 1905 (Costume Research Centre, Bath/photo John Cornwell, Bristol)

24 Mrs Rita de Acosta Lydig (Courtauld Institute of Art, London)

25 Doucet teagown for Réjane. *Les Modes*, Aug 1902 (Costume Research Centre, Bath/photo John Cornwell, Bristol)

26 Doucet dinner gown. *Les Modes*, Jan 1903 (Costume Research Centre, Bath/photo John Cornwell, Bristol)

27 Doeuillet afternoon frock. *Les Modes*, Sept 1904 (Costume Research Centre, Bath/photo John Cornwell, Bristol)

28 Drécoll promenade dress. *Les Modes*, Aug 1905 (Costume Research Centre, Bath/photo John Cornwell, Bristol)

29 Brissaud: Chéruit suit. *La Gazette du Bon Ton*, April 1913 (photo John Freeman & Co.)

30 Redfern's trousseau for Princess Beatrice, American *Harper's Bazar*, 1885. *Victorian Fashions & Costumes from Harper's Bazar: 1867–1898*, Stella Blum ed., Dover Publications, 1974

31 Mary Garden in Redfern town dress. *Les Modes*, Sept 1905 (Costume Research Centre, Bath)

32 John Leech: 'Bloomeriana. A Dream'. *Punch*, vol. 21, 1851 (photo John Freeman & Co.)

33 G.F. Watts: 'Ellen Terry' (National Portrait Gallery)

34 D.G. Rossetti: 'Elizabeth Siddal' (Victoria and Albert Museum)

35 Jane Morris posed by Rossetti (Victoria and Albert Museum)

36 Whistler: 'Mrs F.R. Lelyand', 1873 (copyright of The Frick Collection, New York)

37 G. du Maurier: 'An Impartial Statement in Black and White'. *Punch*, vol. 80, 1881 (photo John Freeman & Co.)

38 W. Frith: 'The Private View at the Royal Academy' (collection of C.J.R. Pope/photo Royal Academy of Arts)

39 Sandoz: Bicycle dress, American *Harper's Bazar*, 1894. *Victorian Fashions & Costumes from Harper's Bazar: 1867–1898*, Stella Blum ed., Dover Publications, 1974

40 Sandoz: Worth teagown, American *Harper's Bazar*, 1891. *Victorian Fashions & Costumes from Harper's Bazar: 1867–1898*, Stella Blum ed., Dover Publications, 1974

41 de Beers: Duchess de la Torre. *The Lady's Realm*, 1896, vol. I (Victoria and Albert Museum)

42 Grecian aesthetic dresses, American *Harper's Bazar*, 1881. *Victorian Fashions & Costumes from Harper's Bazar: 1867–1898*, Stella Blum ed., Dover Publications, 1974

43 Corsets. *La Mode Illustrée*, 1908 (Costume Research Centre, Bath)

44 Paul Iribe, *Les Robes de Paul Poiret* (photo John Freeman & Co.)

45 Hattie Williams in *Decorating Clementine*, 1910 (The Mansell Collection)

46–7 Poiret gowns. *Art et Décoration*, April 1911 (Victoria and Albert Museum)

48 Denise Poiret in *One Thousand and 2 Nights*, 1911. *Poiret* by Palmer White, Studio Vista, 1973

49 Poiret: 'Le Collier Nouveau'. *La Gazette du Bon Ton*, 1914 (photo John Freeman & Co.)

50 'The New Skirt and the Poetry of Motion', *Punch*, vol. 138, 1910 (photo John Freeman & Co.)

51 Poiret mantle. *La Gazette du Bon Ton*, 1920 (photo John Freeman & Co.)

52 Poiret supervising a fitting. *Poiret* by Palmer White, Studio Vista, 1973

90 Lanvin: 'La Fête est Finie'. *La Gazette du Bon Ton*, 1920 (photo John Freeman & Co.)

91 Vionnet: 'La Vitrine'. *La Gazette du Bon Ton*, 1924–5 (photo John Freeman & Co.)

92 Vionnet at work. British *Harper's Bazaar*, Nov 1934 (The National Magazine Company/photo John Freeman & Co.)

93–4 Vionnet Directoire and romantic gowns. British *Vogue*, March 1937 (Victoria and Albert Museum/photos John Freeman & Co.)

95 Alix gown in black jersey. British *Harper's Bazaar*, Feb 1935 (The National Magazine Company/photo John Freeman & Co.)

96 Alix white gown. British *Harper's Bazaar*, 1937 (The National Magazine Company)

97–102 Worth suits 'Suivez-Moi', 'Etincelle', 'Tabac Blond', 'Oui ou Non', 'British court dress' and 'Pleine d'audace' (Worth archive, Victoria and Albert Museum, vols. 1927–28, 1938–39/photos John Freeman & Co.)

103 Worth pyjama suits. *Femina*, 1930 (Costume Research Centre, Bath/photo John Cornwell, Bristol)

104 Patou dining outfits. British *Harper's Bazaar*, Feb 1935 (The National Magazine Company/photo John Freeman & Co.)

105 Patou black crêpe dress. British *Harper's Bazaar*, July 1937 (The National Magazine Company/photo John Freeman & Co.)

106 Evelyne Morris: Duchess of Kent's trousseau from Molyneux. *Illustrated London News*, Dec 1934 (Victoria and Albert Museum)

107 Royal family on the balcony of Buckingham Palace. *Illustrated London News*, May 1935 (Victoria and Albert Museum)

108 Princess Natalie Paley. British *Vogue*, 1928 (The Condé Nast Publications)

109 Two Lelong travel outfits. British *Harper's Bazaar*, March 1932 (The National Magazine Company/photo John Freeman & Co.)

110 Lanvin and Mainbocher dress designs. British *Harper's Bazaar*, Oct 1934 (The National Magazine Company/photo John Freeman & Co.)

111 Mainbocher suit. British *Vogue*, March 1937 (Victoria and Albert Museum)

112 Lily Elsie in *The Merry Widow* (Radio Times Hulton Picture Library)

113 Lucile's model Dolores (American *Vogue*, Sept 1918)

114–15 Lucile designs (The Museum of London)

116 Lucile in 1922 (The Mansell Collection)

117 King George V and Queen Mary in coronation clothes, 1911 (The Museum of London)

118 Olive Hewerdine: Princess Mary's trousseau. *Illustrated London News*, Feb 1922 (Victoria and Albert Museum)

119 Hartnell evening dress, 1933 (courtesy of Sir Norman Hartnell)

120 Queen Elizabeth in 1936 (Fox Photos Ltd)

121 Hartnell's black satin dinner dress. British *Harper's Bazaar*, Dec 1934 (The National Magazine Company/photo John Freeman & Co.)

122 Hartnell suit design 1935 (courtesy of Sir Norman Hartnell)

123 Hartnell evening dress design, 1949 (courtesy of Sir Norman Hartnell)

124 Hardy Amies proto-type Utility model, 1942 (Victoria and Albert Museum)

125 Molyneux grey flannel suit, 1944. British *Vogue*, 1944 (The Condé Nast Publications)

126–9 Hardy Amies coat 'Eminence', 1946, suit 'Easter Sunday', 1949, coat 'Horizon', 1949 and ball gown 'Foam', 1949 (courtesy of Hardy Amies)

130 Charles Creed suit, British *Vogue*, Feb 1938 (The Condé Nast Publications)
131 Angèle Delanghe evening dress. British *Harper's Bazaar*, Nov 1946 (The National Magazine Company/photo John Freeman & Co.)
132 Vivien Leigh in Victor Steibel gown. British *Vogue*, 1937 (The Condé Nast Publications)
133 Victor Steibel studying a fabric. British *Vogue*, Jan 1935 (Costume Research Centre, Bath)
134 Lee: 'Postwar Gowns', *The Evening News*, 1945
135 Contravention of austerity rules. British *Vogue*, Jan 1946 (Victoria and Albert Museum/photo John Freeman & Co.)
136 Two Balmain evening dress designs. British *Harper's Bazaar*, Nov 1947 (The National Magazine Company/photo John Freeman & Co.)
137 Gorau: Balenciaga's straight narrow coat. British *Harper's Bazaar*, Jan/Feb 1946 (The National Magazine Company/photo John Freeman & Co.)
138 Eric: 'The New Look'. British *Vogue*, 1947 (The Condé Nast Publications)
139 Lee: 'The New Look'. *The Evening News*, 1947
140–1 Dior dinner dress and Zerline narrow line. British *Harper's Bazaar*, Oct 1947 (The National Magazine Company/photos John Freeman & Co.)
142 Fath day-cum dinner suit. British *Harper's Bazaar*, Oct 1949 (The National Magazine Company/photo John Freeman & Co.)
143 Balenciaga *fin de journée* suit. British *Harper's Bazaar*, 1946 (The National Magazine Company/photo John Freeman & Co.)

Colour

(between pages 96 and 97)
1 Paul Lacourière, evening gowns. *Journal des Demoiselles*, February 1878. Designed by Mesdemoiselles Vidal of 42 rue Vivienne, and made on sewing machines from Wheeler and Wilson. (Collection: Courtauld Institute of Art)
2 Paul Lacourière, visiting toilette. *Journal des Demoiselles*, September 1879. Designs by Mademoiselle Tarot. (Collection: Courtauld Institute of Art)
3 Paquin town dress for summer 1910 (Victoria and Albert Museum).
4 T. Holden, summer *toilette de ville*. *Les Grandes Modes de Paris*, c.1912. (Collection: Courtauld Institute of Art)
5 T. Holden, *toilette de bal*. Designed by Laferrière. *Les Grandes Modes de Paris*, c.1912. (Collection: Courtauld Institute of Art)
6 Paul Iribe. *Les Robes de Paul Poiret*, 1908. (Collection: Courtauld Institute of Art)
7 A.E. Marty, *Le Nid de Pinsons*. *Gazette du Bon Ton*, 1922. (Collection: Courtauld Institute of Art)
8 A.E. Marty. *La Glace ou un Coup D'Oeil en Passant*. *Gazette du Bon Ton*, 1922. (Collection: Courtauld Institute of Art)

1 The Rise of the Couturier: Worth, the First Fashion Dictator

Until the late seventeenth century the professional business of making clothes for ladies in the upper reaches of society was mainly in the hands of men. It was the tailor who made court gowns, fashionable townswear and riding habits. In London in the 1660s, for example, Mr Unthankes of the Strand was tailor to both the Countess of Castlemaine and to Mrs Samuel Pepys. Many households of course had their sewing women who made underwear and children's clothes, or who carried out alterations, but the grander items in the wardrobe were obtained from the tailor. Lower down the social scale women made their own clothes, while the poor had to rely on the enormous market in old and second-hand clothing.[1]

In Paris in 1675 a law was passed which was to change this pattern completely. After serving three years' apprenticeship in cutting and dressmaking, women were now permitted to go into business as *couturières*, that is, as seamstresses.[2] There were to be four categories of dressmaker: the *couturière en habit* made women's clothes, the *couturière en corps d'enfant* specialized in children's clothing, the *couturière en linge* made linenwear and the *couturière en garniture* created the trimmings. Slowly over the years more and more women became dressmakers, until the whole business of making clothes for ladies was virtually a female monopoly, although tailors continued to make riding habits and many corset-makers would be men. Gradually this new pattern expanded from France into neighbouring countries, and the dressmaker became a person of some importance in the world of fashion.

Undoubtedly the most famous of these dressmakers was Mlle Rose Bertin, who made clothes for Queen Marie-Antoinette. Strictly speaking, Mlle Bertin was not a *couturière* but a *marchande de modes*, for she sold bonnets, fans, frills and lace as well as making garments, but she was famous enough in her day to be regarded as something of a minister for fashion. Her customers included princesses and duchesses in Paris, London, Madrid and St Petersburg. At this period a fashion was still launched at court, and before she left Austria, Marie-Antoinette was instructed by her mother, the Empress Maria Theresia, to always set the style herself. This she proceeded to do with the help of Mlle Bertin, and a flood of fashions for dresses, hats and fichus emanated from the court of Versailles in the 1780s.[3] Rose Bertin did not create such fashions single-handed: rather they were the outcome of discussions between the queen and her ladies and were then realized by Bertin as actual items of wear. Thus Rose Bertin does not qualify for the title of fashion dictator in the sense of being a completely independent operator who launches new lines at her own establishment, regardless of the opinions of her customers.

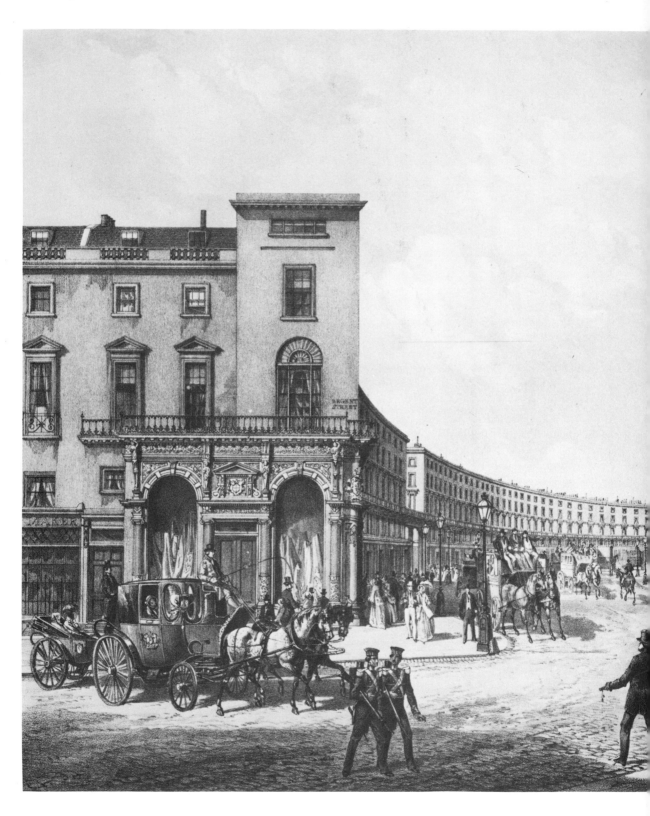

2 The Quadrant, Regent Street, London, now Piccadilly Circus, showing Swan and Edgar's on the left, where Worth worked and lived from 1838 to 1845. Lithograph by E. Walker.

Fashion was still something of a team enterprise at the court of Napoleon I. The ceremonial wear was designed by artists such as David and Isabey, and the fashionable wear by Garnerey, to be then made up by the tailor, Leroy. In fact Leroy was good enough as a tailor to oust the female dressmaker for the time being. It was he who made clothes for the Empress Josephine, Empress Marie-Louise, Countess Marie Walewska and even, in 1814 – politics no barrier – the Duchess of Wellington. But Leroy was never a fashion designer: he merely carried out the ideas devised for him by artists.[4]

After the downfall of Napoleon, the dressmaker resumed her importance as the principal creator of female dress. During the 1830s in Paris Mme Delatour was making the wardrobe for Queen Marie-Amélie, and by the time of the Second Napoleonic Empire in the 1850s Mmes Vignon, Palmyre and Rodger were the dressmakers to the new young Empress Eugénie. This female monopoly would have continued but for the advent of one man, and an Englishman at that. Charles Frederick Worth was not only to break into that female trade by becoming a dressmaker, but to change its nature and status completely by becoming the first of the great fashion dictators. Worth was not only to launch fashions at court, but to continue to launch fashions after that court had disappeared into history, as a totally independent authority in his own right. As such he created a new art.

Worth was born in the small south Lincolnshire town of Bourne on 13 October 1825.[5] He came from a professional background, his grandfather, father and brother all being solicitors, but this comfortable security was shattered in 1836 when Charles Frederick was eleven. His father had long had a weakness for drinking and gambling which that year led to disaster, for he lost all his money and was no longer able to support his family. It therefore fell to the mother, Mary Worth, to find a way out of ruin. Her elder son was safely embarked on his legal training, but there was now no hope of a professional career for the younger boy. Mrs Worth herself had to undertake work as a housekeeper for some cousins, and the best she could do for young Charles Frederick was to find him a job with a printer.[6] The boy endured the work for one year, but found it very dirty and boring. He entreated his mother to find him something better, but the choice was very limited. If he was not to be sent into a factory or the forces, where could he go but into trade? If Charles Frederick showed the least interest in fabrics, the best solution would be to apprentice him to a draper or a milliner. There he would receive his keep, and the work would be clean. In 1838 Mary Worth took her son to London and apprenticed him to the drapers, Swan and Edgar, in Piccadilly Circus. He was a country boy no more.

Between 1838 and 1845 Worth grew up in the midst of the metropolis, at the very centre of the fashionable London world. The area contained the best shops in town, selling the most expensive lines in fabrics and accessories, and the leading milliners' salons, as dressmakers were then known. It was the custom then for a lady to purchase the material she wanted for a dress at one of the textile houses and to take it to her milliner to have it made up into a gown. Worth was trained to specialize in the sale of fabrics to such customers, and he thereby acquired a great knowledge of and

→→→A PROSPECT·OF·A·FASHYONABLE·HABERDASHER hys·SHOPE·

experience in handling textiles, in appreciating their qualities and in judging which sorts were best suited for particular types of dress. Such a sound education was to be invaluable to him later in life and it was to colour his approach to dress design, for he always started with the nature of the fabric itself.

During his apprenticeship Worth made some attempt to compensate for the end of his formal education. He read the latest novelists such as Bulwer Lytton, and when he was out on errands, would drop into the new National Gallery to study the paintings. He had no tutor to guide his appreciation, and what attracted him to pictures was their representation of textiles, their use of colour and their illustration of past styles in costume. He could begin to see for himself that certain aspects of contemporary female fashion were revivals of modes from the past, and this was to give him an insight into the nature of dress design. He could perceive what inspired the setters of fashion in Paris.

Once his seven-year apprenticeship was over, Worth took up employ-

3 The environment in which Worth worked for twelve hours a day, with all the shop assistants dressed up like dandies, a seat for every customer, and a footman at the door to assist ladies in and out of their carriages and drive off beggars.

ment at the finest silk mercers in Regent Street, Lewis and Allenby, purveyors to Queen Victoria. He did not remain there long, however, for he had made up his mind that he ought to see the centre of international high fashion for himself. London might be the capital of masculine styles, but it was Paris which set the styles for ladies. As Worth was dealing almost exclusively with female customers the idea was a very sensible one, but the problem was how to achieve it. As he had only just started to earn his living he had very little capital of his own, and had to appeal to his mother to help him with the fare. This she did, and Charles Frederick Worth arrived in Paris at the age of twenty with £5 in his pocket.

Now Worth probably knew all the French terms employed in the textile business and he may have taught himself some basic grammar, but this did not equip him to qualify for employment in one of the leading fabric shops, where a fluent command of colloquial French was essential. In fact two years were to pass before he got back into selling materials. He had a very difficult time to begin with, doing odd jobs, but in 1846 he was taken on by a dry goods store, and this gave him the opportunity to acquire fluent sales talk in French. Twelve months later he was back in the fashionable world, working as a sales assistant for the most famous mercers in Paris, Gagelin. Here he was to remain for nearly twelve years, graduating to the post of *premier commis* (leading salesman).

Initially Worth was doing the same work as he had done in London, selling fabrics, but by 1849 his employers were using him to sell shawls and mantles. These were the only items of ready-made clothing that were sold by high-class shops, and at Gagelin such articles were displayed by girls known as *demoiselles de magasin*, who were a kind of model. Worth came to work with one girl above all, Marie Vernet, and in time a romance blossomed between them. Their relationship was to be the catalyst which set Worth off on a new course. As he had to sell the shawls which Marie modelled, he came to take an interest in her appearance, and this led him to start making her some dresses. To display a shawl to the best advantage the model's dress ought to be kept relatively plain, and Worth created for Marie very simple dresses in white muslin to serve as a background to silken finery. His lady customers noticed these plain but very elegant creations, and began to ask him to make such dresses for themselves. Shop assistants worked such very long hours, however, that it was not possible for Worth to take on such orders himself. He asked his employers if he might not start a small dressmaking department in the shop, but they refused outright, declaring that Gagelin were famous mercers, not common dressmakers! It was unheard of for a fabric house to make women's dresses. Nevertheless, customers continued to press their demands, and by 1850 Gagelin gave in. Worth was given his new department together with a small team of seamstresses. Thus, almost by chance, he came to be a male dressmaker.

The new department flourished, with Worth himself as the cutter-in-chief. His intimate knowledge of textiles, together with an appreciation of English tailoring techniques, combined to create dresses where fabric and construction were in harmony. Not for him gowns where the design took no account of the material to be used; for Worth the design depended on the

LE MONITEUR DE LA MODE

4 Pelisse wrap by Gagelin on the left, as worn by Marie Worth as a shop model. Fashion plate by Jules David.

nature of the stuff itself. Consequently his creations set a new standard for dressmaking. Their fit was perfection, their finish unparalleled. Here was the foundation of a new art, the creation of clothes which were perfect in every way, clothes which were haute couture. Gagelin were sufficiently impressed with Worth's achievement to include some of his dresses in their exhibit at the Great Exhibition in London in 1851. Their display was rewarded with success and the firm was presented with a prize medal, the jury report praising Worth's dresses for their elegant style.[7] Gagelin followed this up by exhibiting some more Worths at the Exposition Universelle in Paris in 1855, and once again were awarded a first-class medal.[8] Of particular interest was Worth's design for a court train. Instead of suspending the train from the waist of a gown as was then usual, he made it fall from the shoulders, thereby allowing for a greater sweep of material with more room for elaborate embroidery. This type of court train was later to be adopted by courts across Europe.

Thus within four years Worth's creations had won prizes at two international exhibitions, so there could be no doubt about his genius for dress design. These exhibitions widened Worth's horizons for they had attracted enormous crowds of foreign visitors to London and Paris. Railways were rapidly spreading across Europe and the United States, and steam ships were now making regular crossings of the Atlantic, so that movement between countries was suddenly on a scale undreamt of when Worth was a boy. Such developments in transport meant a new flood of foreign buyers: Americans could now shop in Paris. Worth had the sense to respond to this new phenomenon, and to cater for it.

When a dressmaker showed her latest creations at her salon, she presented each design in one fabric only. Worth went beyond this and showed his dresses in a variety of fabrics, thereby allowing buyers greater freedom of choice. If they did not care for velvet, then the same dress was available in silk, satin or tulle. There was no need for them to go to another dressmaker's in search of an alternative; Worth had it all under one roof. Moreover his clothes for export were of the same high quality as those for his French customers, and not the indifferent articles usually produced for foreigners. The foreign buyers going to Worth were assured of excellence, and this they appreciated.

Also of unprecedented importance was Worth's relation with the French textile industry. He was not a dressmaker who went to a fabric shop and could buy only what it had to offer; his department was in a mercer's, so he was meeting the sales representatives of the silk mills in Lyon in person. Consequently he could begin to exert an influence over the placing of orders. He could tell the salesmen what patterns and materials he required, and explain what colours he wanted developed. Thus textile manufacturers began to respond to Worth's suggestions, and to suit some of their products to his requirements. Such a direct relationship did not exist between the woman dressmaker and the industry. Wherever he turned, Worth was transforming dressmaking in the quality of its creations, the quantity of its output, and the scale of its operations.

It might be thought that Gagelin would have cherished such an asset, but they did not. To them Worth was never more than a leading salesman. When he asked his employers for a place on the board, he was refused. This rejection, together with Gagelin's lack of consideration for Marie, made Worth profoundly dissatisfied. He and Marie had married in 1851, and two sons were born to them: Gaston in 1853 and Jean-Philippe in 1856. Gagelin had expected Marie to continue working right to the end of her pregnancies, and never made any allowances for her rest or comfort. By 1858 Worth had had enough. He knew another leading salesman, Otto Bobergh, a Swede, who was also tired of his employers, and the two men agreed to go into partnership. Bobergh raised a loan, and the new dressmaking establishment of Worth et Bobergh opened at 7 rue de la Paix that same year.

There had been several remarkable changes in the French political structure during all this time. Since Worth first arrived in Paris, the country had changed from a monarchy, to a republic, and then to an empire, within the space of four years. Paris was now the capital of the Second Empire with Napoleon III on the throne. The city itself was being transformed by Baron

Haussmann with enormous boulevards and new quarters. The Napoleonic family were great believers in glory, and Napoleon III was no exception. He set a pattern of splendour which made other European capitals appear dull and staid. Entertaining became a veritable industry, with state balls, ministerial and ambassadorial functions, imperial receptions, military parades, state visits, and gala performances of opera and ballet. At the summit of this glittering assemblage was the beautiful Empress Eugénie, whose elegance and style gave a new impetus to French fashion. What she wore, other women copied. Whilst he could not have foreseen such developments, nor such an empress, Worth could not have been better placed for a dressmaker to flourish.

Success was but modest to begin with. Some Worth gowns did make an appearance at court, but what the firm lacked was a customer of outstanding social importance. To attain fame and fortune it was essential that Worth et Bobergh should be patronized by a lady of the highest rank and influence, who would wear their creations at the smartest gatherings. Such a need was to be felt by every couture house. It was answered for Worth et Bobergh in December 1859 when a new Austrian ambassador was appointed to Paris, Prince Richard von Metternich. Early in 1860 at the very start of the fashionable season, Worth et Bobergh decided to approach his wife. Since it would have been very irregular for Worth to approach the princess about her clothes himself, for a dressmaker was by definition a woman, he sent his wife with an album of designs. At first Princess Metternich could not be bothered to see her, and when she was told that Worth was a man and English, she considered the whole idea too preposterous to want to have anything to do with it. Eventually she did glance at the album, was delighted with what she saw, and allowed Marie Worth to be presented. Mme Worth explained that her husband and his partner were most anxious for the honour of making some dresses for the princess, and asked her to name her own price. Princess Metternich said she would be pleased to order two dresses, one for morning and one for evening, and that they were not to cost more than 300 francs each.[9]

This was an enormous stroke of luck. Pauline von Metternich was a person of the highest nobility and a very energetic and commanding personality, who was rapidly to become a dominant figure at the French Court. If Worth could please her, it could open the door to regular aristocratic patronage. The opportunity was worth some financial risk, so he made the evening dress from a very expensive new material, of white silk tulle woven with silver. After only one fitting the dress was ready, and the princess declared that she had rarely seen a gown that was lovelier or better made. She wore it to the next ball at the Palais des Tuileries. What happened then was beyond Worth's wildest dreams. Before the ball the emperor and empress greeted the *corps diplomatique*, and when they came to the Metternichs the Empress Eugénie asked the princess straight away who had made her a dress of such elegant simplicity. Princess Metternich replied that the maker was an Englishman named Worth. 'Very well,' said the empress, 'kindly have him instructed to report to me tomorrow morning at 10 o'clock.' Worth and Bobergh were standing on the threshold of the greatest

possible success.

They nearly ruined the opportunity. The gown the empress had admired was in tulle; they responded to her order with a dress of beige brocade. There were probably two reasons why they chose brocade: it was a very luxurious fabric, and it would please the textile manufacturers in Lyon if the empress could be persuaded to wear more of their products (with some benefit to Worth on the side). But when Worth delivered the dress to the Empress Eugénie, it was almost a disaster. The empress regarded the gown and stated that it looked like curtain material. She did not like brocade. Worth hastily tried to persuade her that she could start a fashion for Lyon brocade, but the empress was not interested. All would have been lost but for the entry of the Emperor Napoleon III at that very moment. Keeping his wits about him Worth was clever enough to try a political argument. He appealed to the emperor, saying that as Lyon was a very republican city, would it not benefit the imperial cause if the empress would agree to wear more fabrics from Lyon? Napoleon III agreed. He told the empress she need only wear the brocade gown once or twice, to encourage the Lyon textile trade, but wear it she must.

Worth was saved by the skin of his teeth, and he had gained a double advantage. Not only could he make dresses for the empress which she herself liked, but he could get her to wear something which she did not like if he could convince her that it would help industry. Such gowns the empress dubbed her 'political dresses'.[10] This meant of course that manufacturers would strive their hardest to persuade Worth to promote their products at court, and gave him immense patronage within the trade. Such a connection with industry was way beyond anything which the ordinary dressmaker possessed. After this Worth never put a foot wrong. Each dress he created for the empress was so lovely that in 1864 she gave him the monopoly of supplying all her evening and state wear. Worth was never the empress's sole dressmaker, for some of her day wear came from other *couturières*, but he controlled the most important and luxurious part of her wardrobe.

Worth was the imperial dressmaker. From then on his prices were the highest in all Paris. His cheapest frock cost as much as an evening gown elsewhere, but princesses and duchesses flocked to the rue de la Paix because Worth dressed the empress and all her ladies. People were astounded at the expense involved, and only then did the world wake up to what Worth had achieved. Here was a man making clothes for the best dressed empress in Europe. Immediately other men tried to copy his success, and Charles Dickens reported the development in his weekly journal, *All the Year Round*:

... would you believe that, in the latter half of the nineteenth century, there are bearded milliners – man-milliners, authentic men, like Zouaves – who, with their solid fingers, take the exact dimensions of the highest titled women in Paris – robe them, unrobe them, and make them turn backward and forward before them ...[11]

Such rivals soon faded away, but what a shock it was to the mid-nineteenth century that a man should be making dresses on women, seeing them in a state of undress, touching their bodies, and ordering them to parade before

5 The answer to Worth's prayers, Princess Pauline von Metternich, who promoted his clothes at the French imperial court and was a dominant fashion leader. Unfinished portrait by Degas.

him. Moralists were appalled. They declared that Maison Worth et Bobergh must be a house of orgies. Poor Marie Worth was very distressed by such criticism, but it did not last long, for the press came to realize that Worth was not a sex fiend. The imperial dressmaker was not even a tradesman; Worth was a gentleman – '. . . a perfect gentleman, always fresh shaved, always frizzled. Black coat, white cravat, and batiste shirt-cuffs fastened at the wrists with golden buttons, he officiates with all the gravity of a diplomatist,'[12] wrote Dickens. Soon Worth had his own coat-of-arms and was building himself a luxury villa just outside Paris, where he was visited by such great persons as Princess Metternich, Princess Mathilde Bonaparte, and the British ambassador and his wife.[13] The payment of such honours to a dressmaker was unheard of. Some sophisticates might scoff at his *nouveau riche* décor, but here was a gentleman of business on terms of social intimacy with the nobility.

Moreover Worth was not just a businessman. He said that he was an artist, for he did not make dresses: he 'composed toilettes'. In time he even came to dress more like an artist, with a Rembrandt beret and a floppy cravat like Wagner (see fig 1). Such an attitude, of being an artist, was considered outrageous in some quarters. Worth was subjected to a vicious attack by Hippolyte Taine, who mocked him by putting the following words into his mouth: 'I am a great artist, I have Delacroix's sense of colour. . . . Art is God, and the bourgeoisie was made to take our orders.'[14] The sight of a dressmaker giving himself serious airs made some critics very angry. Fashion was a frivolous subject, so how could a dressmaker be taken seriously? But Worth took it very seriously. So keen was he to raise the study of dress to a new level that he adopted a completely unprecedented attitude towards his customers. A lady did not go to Maison Worth as she would to an ordinary dressmaker and say that she wanted a dress in green silk by Friday. First she made an appointment (for Worth was an extremely busy man), which was most unusual, and when admitted to his presence she would find that her own ideas counted for nothing. Worth would study her, note her colouring, her hair, her jewels, her style, and then he would design a gown which he thought suited her. Anyone going to Worth had to submit to his taste, while his overseas customers had to rely on his taste completely. It did not matter if they were the Empress Marie Feodorovna in St Petersburg or Mrs J. Pierpoint Morgan in New York, they were sent what Worth judged would suit them best.

Such dictatorship from a dressmaker was unprecedented. Some attributed it to arrogance on Worth's part, but the philosophy behind such dictation to the customer was to create a house style and a standard of excellence. If Worth controlled the final product, no woman could ruin his design by wearing the wrong hat or the wrong shawl; thus the reputation of his house was sustained. This control was so absolute that before a state ball Princess Metternich and other ladies would report to Worth at 10 p.m. They would wait in a drawing room with *pâté de foie* and madeira for refreshment, and one by one be ushered into the presence of the great designer, so that he might make the finishing touches. The princess declared that his last inspection was essential for she would not have felt dressed without it.[15]

Thus Worth became the supreme arbiter of taste in dress. His judgements were reported in the press and read by both the aristocracy and the middle classes. His name was known as no *couturière's* had ever been. The Second Empire, which had made Worth rich, collapsed in 1870 before the Prussian attack, and Worth was forced to close, but he reopened in 1871 and continued to thrive and expand under the new Third Republic, sustained by courts in Europe and by millionaires in the United States. Here was a new phenomenon, a fashion house which did not rely on one native court for its principal customers, but which had an international clientele of considerable proportions. In addition, Worth model dresses and patterns were purchased by American dressmakers and shops in great numbers, to be reproduced for the wider market, providing him with a rich income.

Charles Frederick Worth would not have thrived without the technological developments of the day. For instance, the scale of his international dressmaking was only possible through the growth of railway, steamship and telegraph systems. Also, Maison Worth could not have turned out hundreds of ball gowns a week, without the improvement in sewing machines to do most of the seams; the finishing, of course, was still done by hand. By 1871 he had a staff of 1,200, which was a very different scale of business from the dressmaker with a few dozen seamstresses in her attics. It was Worth who turned dressmaking into big business: he found Paris with a craft and left it with an industry. Compared with him Bertin and Leroy were provincial in the scale of their operations. He undoubtedly transformed the role of the dress designer, giving it new power and status. When he died in 1895 he had held a monopoly of some thirty-five years over the fashion world; no couturier since has had such total dominion. Moreover, the pattern he established was to last a hundred years. In the words of the future couturier, Poiret, 'le grand Worth' was 'l'instituteur de l'industrie de la grande couture.'

2 Worth and Fashion

Fashion is *une façon*, a way of doing things – in other words, a style. Subtle changes of fashion can be seen in many cultures, but why there is such a force for very marked changes of style in Western culture is perhaps due to the following reasons. First, there is competition: J.C. Flügel, writing in 1930, considered social and sexual competition to be the essential cause of fashion.[1] Thus a woman follows fashion by altering her appearance to accord with the latest definition of beauty, because she wants to show that she is rich enough to change her wardrobe often, and because she wishes to appear more attractive than her contemporaries. Certainly this is a view of which followers of fashion have not been unaware. Back in 1661 Lady Wright declared that the great happiness of being in the fashion was to show scorn for those who were not, such as citizens' wives and country gentlewomen.[2] This is in fact competition between classes. Two hundred years later when Worth was asked the reason why women took so much trouble over dress, he thought the answer was obvious. It was for the pleasure of being smart and for the greater joy of snuffing out competition from other women.[3]

Such a view is very appropriate to the nineteenth century, for this was a time when new money from industry and banking was making it possible for the middle classes to challenge the aristocracy as never before. Industrial wealth could now outrank landed wealth, and one feature of the French court during the Second Empire was the appearance of manufacturing millionaires and international bankers at its functions. What was unusual about this new class was that the men concentrated their energies on making more money and did not spend so much of it on their personal wardrobes as the aristocracy had done. The man left it to his wife to display his monetary power by spending his money: her life of elegant leisure advertised his social status.[4] Worth's success depended on this phenomenon after the fall of the Empire, for what better way was there for a millionaire to show that he had 'arrived' than to send his wife to the most expensive dressmaker in the world, the man who clothed empresses?

Another form of competition, which very much affects fashion in the twentieth century, is the economic. The closer couture becomes connected with industry, through being bought up by manufacturers or international corporations, the greater the reason to introduce changes in styles for purely financial considerations. Worth began it with his promotion of Lyon textiles. Since then international textile firms and agencies such as the Wool Secretariat have tried to persuade couturiers to make greater use of their particular products in order to increase sales. Such pressures are less concerned with the development of a particular fashion to its individual fulfillment at its own pace.

A second cause of fashion changes can be seen in man's desire for change itself, an interest in novelty which R. König has termed *neophilia*.[5] Part of this interest is expressed by the changes which take place in relations between the generations. Each generation likes to think that it is different from the preceding one, that it has new ways of looking at problems, new attitudes towards moral questions, and is more aware of new developments; and the best way for it to illustrate this difference is by dressing differently and living in a different décor. Obviously there are great variations in this expression of difference. At some periods change is gradual and can be seen in subtle variations in fashion and not in the complete abandonment of a style of living. At other periods change is more marked and more blatantly displayed, as in the adoption of a form of dress that appears revolutionary. Change in dress is then part of the expression of this process.

Within this framework, and closely connected with the competitive element, there is the need for the dressmaker to have something new for her clients if she is to stay in business. Any modification in a dress, any addition or subtraction which can make last year's dress appear old by the mere fact of this year's being new, will attract a customer's interest. Thus, to the customer, to have something new is looked upon as good enough reason for buying it, whether one needs it or not, for it puts the buyer a little ahead of her peers. To respond to and satisfy this feeling for novelty was an essential duty of a couturier, as Worth himself said: 'My business is not only to execute but especially to invent. My invention is the secret of my success. I don't want people to invent for themselves; if they did, I should lose half my trade.'[6] Marie Worth, who was the first to wear many of her husband's creations, agreed that this was indeed so.

What was regarded as suitable conduct for a woman in 1850 was giving way to a very different attitude by 1900, and to yet another by 1920. The couturier had to keep up with such developments, and indeed anticipate them if he was to retain the loyalty of his clientele.

Such then are some of the forces which contribute to the existence of fashion. Those fashions which Worth himself introduced were varied, and his achievement has been much clouded by legend. He was so famous that later generations have regarded him as the originator of every fashion from 1850 to the 1890s, which has resulted in a very confused picture. Foremost among the errors is that Worth invented the crinoline and introduced it to the Empress Eugénie. *Punch* reported that the vogue for crinolines, or 'crinolinomania', was begun by Eugénie in 1856.[7] Worth did not meet the empress until 1860, so there is no question that he could have persuaded her to adopt crinolines four years before. As for inventing the crinoline, one must first ask which sort of crinoline is meant, for there were a great many varieties. In the 1840s when Worth was still an apprentice, a crinoline petticoat was being worn, made of horse hair, as the French term *crin* implies, in order to give skirts greater width. As fashion came to demand even greater expansion, such petticoats were stiffened and held out by cane ribs or metal bands. In the mid-1850s the flexible steel frame appeared, which in France was known as a *cage*. Women took to it with delight, for it liberated their legs from the weight of petticoats. Such *cages* had their

6 Worth at Gagelin. His early experiment with the crinoline, wide rather than bell-shaped, which did not become the dominant style. The falling lace collar and slashed sleeves were characteristic of Worth's use of historical features in fashionable dress, but the overall design is much simpler than the fussy products of his contemporaries. Plate by Jules David.

problems in management, but they did enable the woman of the 1850s to feel more mobile than the heavily laden woman of the 1840s.

There were dozens of different sorts of crinoline, by as many makers, each claiming to be bigger or better than its rivals. It was in fact the first truly industrial fashion, for there were factories which made nothing but crinoline *cages* and shops which sold nothing else, as Mayhew reported.[8] Worth certainly adopted the crinoline *cage* early, for among the advertisements for his clothes published by Gagelin in *Le Moniteur de la Mode* in 1852/3 there is an extremely wide dress, termed a '*grande nouveauté*'. It is in fact much wider than the bell-shaped crinolines which came to dominate the 1850s, and is a version which did not take on. Thus Worth's first type of crinoline was not a success although it was a prototype of the wider crinolines which came into fashion by 1860.

Where Worth was acclaimed for his dealings with the crinoline *cage* was in 1864, when he was the court couturier. The great size of the skirts made it impossible for a lady to hold her husband's arm, for it occupied a considerable area. Worth decided that the *cage* had gone too far, and launched his reform. He flattened the skirt in front and pushed all the fullness towards the back. Mme Carette, one of the empress's ladies-in-waiting, declared that Worth had delivered women from the tyranny of the *cage* by introducing his crinoline.[9] When she arrived at court in 1864 his narrower skirt had replaced the voluminous hoop. This then was Worth's variation on the crinoline, and not the invention of the principle.

Another modern myth has it that Worth created the dress for the Empress Eugénie in the famous group portrait by Winterhalter, of the empress with her ladies in 1855.[10] There is no documentary evidence to support this view. Granted that at that time the empress's dressmakers bought materials at Gagelin, where Worth was the leading salesman, and that it is possible that he sold them the actual fabric to be seen in the portrait, it would nevertheless be wishful thinking to believe that the imperial dressmakers would have handed over their commission for a dress which would be immortalized in a painting to a new and unknown rival dressmaker, and a man at that. Competitors are not usually so obliging. It was another five years before the empress summoned Worth.

Once Worth became imperial couturier in 1860 he had to submit to the

7 Worth's future customers, Empress Eugénie with her ladies, painted by Winterhalter in 1855.

traditional method for launching fashions at court. He would take designs to Princess Metternich and the empress's ladies for them to be discussed, and then those suggestions which had been approved would be submitted to the empress for her opinion. Once they were all in agreement over a new style, Worth would have the costume made up and it would be launched in public by Princess Metternich or one of the court beauties, when driving through the Bois. If the design did not create a scandal, then the empress herself would wear it, and this was a virtual decree that other fashionable women should follow suit.

The earliest fashion which Worth launched in this way was the shorter skirt. The empress was very fond of long country walks and of promenading by the sea, but found ground-length skirts a hinderance. It would not do for an empress to hitch her skirt up like a *cantinière* so Worth was asked to provide a solution. He therefore devised a walking skirt which reached only to the ankle, thus freeing the feet, while keeping the legs modestly concealed. At first there was some criticism that this style was too daring, but the empress and her ladies were in favour, and soon common sense ruled that this skirt was the most practical for excursions.

The shoulder-hung court train which Worth had shown at the 1855 exhibition soon ousted the waist-hung train from European courts, and could be seen as far apart as London and St Petersburg. It allowed for

8 Worth's first fashion for Empress Eugénie, the walking skirt, practical but modest. The empress, in white in the centre of the group of ladies, is wearing it for a seaside promenade. 'The Beach at Trouville' by L. Boudin, 1863.

elaborate ornamentation with gold and silver embroidery upon velvet, and was often lined luxuriously with lace or cloth of silver. Worth advertised this style in the Paris trade journal for 1868, and was able to ensure its success by sending examples whenever foreign customers asked for court wear.

Worth's first evening gown for Princess Metternich had been in white, a fabric which he made highly fashionable in the 1860s. He would build up an effect of richness by throwing clouds of tulle over heavier stuffs, such as amber tulle embroidered with golden flowers and arabesques over a skirt of amber satin. French court dress for ladies was white evening dress, but Worth was able to provide variety by changing the trimmings. Empress Eugénie's evening gowns were white tulle caught by violets, her favourite flower, or by ivy leaves or gold fringes. Such simple effects were very characteristic of Worth's style, and enabled him to launch some new fashions very easily. Foremost among these was the tunic dress. This consisted simply of a knee-length gown worn over a long skirt, but it provided ample opportunity for variations of material. A lace tunic could be worn over a long silk skirt, or a velvet tunic over a brocade skirt, or a tulle tunic over a satin skirt. It was the creation of a master designer, producing striking effects by simple means. This style affected both day and evening wear, and lasted well into the 1870s. Sometimes the tunic style was termed a peplum or an apron skirt, but they were all variations on the same theme – a short skirt over a long one.

Given Worth's reputation for the excellent fit of his clothes, it is not surprising that he did not like to see his feeling for line being swamped by additional clutter. The target of his criticism was the shawl or mantle, with which nineteenth-century ladies were accustomed to drape themselves whenever they went outdoors, for it was considered indecent to show the female shape above the waist in the street. To abolish shawls at one fell

9 Empress Eugénie wearing Worth's tunic dress in an evening variation. She is accompanied by Czar Alexander II of Russia in male court dress with kneebreeches, and followed by the King of Prussia and Napoleon III. Detail from the painting by Tetar van Elven, 1867.

10 The demure woman of the 1840s, her vision blinkered by the bonnet. Drawing by Constantin Guys.

stroke would have been too sensational, but Worth did persuade women to lighten them. He did so by sending his wife and Princess Metternich to the races at Longchamp with only gauze and lace over their shoulders. Such simplicity made all the other women appear overdressed, and by the next opening of the races no shawls were to be seen on the fashionable set. This change was of great importance in making fitted outdoor clothes respectable again, and the 1860s saw the return of fitted coats and jackets for ladies.

Another fussy effect which Worth removed was the *bavolet*, the frill at the back of the bonnet which concealed a woman's neck. He not only persuaded his wife to go without a *bavolet*, but he also persuaded her to wear hats instead of bonnets.[11] The bonnet had dominated feminine heads since the end of the eighteenth century to such an extent that hats were looked upon as too sporty and masculine for respectable ladies, but once Mrs Worth and Princess Metternich dared to appear in hats at Longchamp, attitudes began to change. Slowly but surely the hat replaced the bonnet during the 1860s, and the shape of the female head could be seen in public, instead of just two eyes and a nose peering out from the depths of a bonnet, bows, and *bavolet*. Worth's use of Longchamp was extremely important in providing future couturiers with a recognizable location at which to introduce new fashions. The racecourse, modelled on English examples, was opened in 1859, and

11 The bolder woman of the 1860s, but swamped in shawls and bonnets with *bavolets*. Drawing by Constantin Guys.

Worth was the first couturier to use this gathering of fashionable society as his launching ground. In so doing he established a tradition which couturiers were to follow for nearly a hundred years.

Worth's most sensational fashion of course was his abolition of the *cage-crinoline* in 1864. It attracted a storm of controversy, for women had been wearing voluminous skirts since the 1830s, so the reversion to a narrower line, suggestive of the actual female form beneath, was considered almost indecent exposure. Nevertheless narrower skirts were such an improvement upon enormous *cage*-crinolines, with one lady no longer occupying the whole width of a pavement, that the attacks from moralists were overcome. There still remained one problem, however, for if one got rid of the *cage* it meant that the dress itself was now too long. Worth pushed such surplus material to the back, and for the next few years dresses with very long trains were fashionable for daytime as well as for evening. Yet this fashion was not

12 Worth's flat-fronted crinoline of 1864 with all the fullness pushed to the back. This is another example of his tunic dress, with a dark blue velvet tunic worn over a light blue silk skirt, showing the elegant simplicity of which he was a master.

without its difficulties, since trains could be trodden on or fallen over, so in 1869 Worth decided to tame it. From his study of art he knew that in the past there had been emphasis upon the back of the figure as a fashionable feature. Moreover he was very fond of late seventeenth-century styles when a horse hair pad over the rear had been the foundation for an elaborate arrangement of drapery cascading into a train. He therefore took his idea and adapted it to suit nineteenth-century taste, raising the waistline to accord with the current higher waist known as the Josephine, and sweeping the train up over a more pronounced pad of horsehair, called a *tournure*, and later to be termed a bustle. Upon this structure it was possible to erect a multitude of decorative devices, with swags of drapery, festoons of lace, rows of ribbon and countless tiers of frills and fringes, in a waterfall of fancies. Here the sweeping back of skirts attained its apogee: this was as far as that fashion could develop.

The collapse of the Second Empire in 1870 did not result in the collapse of fashion, and by 1873 Worth was launching new styles in his own right, completely free of any court supervision. That year he introduced a wider train for evening, his fan train, consisting of three deep pleats in the skirt where it fell from the bustle, causing the material to spread out on the floor.

13 Cartoon by Bertall claiming that Worth's pushing material to the back of a dress would result in enormous trains, 1864.

14 Worth's introduction of the *tournure* or bustle in 1869, as worn by his customer Mélanie Comtesse de Pourtalès, who later autographed the photograph as a present to Worth's son, Jean-Philippe, in memory of old times.

More significantly that year he brought about the demise of the tunic dress and overskirt, by making bodice and skirt as one without any waist seam. This was a style which depended upon construction above all, for the fit was achieved by long darts in the bodice, built upon a boned lining, resulting in a firm composition called a cuirass. Here the tailoring skills for which Maison Worth was famous were used to the full, for such dresses were as precisely

15 Evening toilette with Worth's fan train, in black Chambéry gauze with gold-coloured stripes over black silk, and trimmed with roses of chenille and silk in scarlet, yellow and black, 1873.

16 Worth export model as copied by Lord and Taylor of New York for licensed reproduction. Cuirass bodice abolishes tunic top and waist seam in favour of a longer line. Black silk trimmed with velvet, silk and fringe, and full trained skirt, 1874.

engineered as any machine. The fabric had to fit upon the foundation from neck to hip without so much as a wrinkle or pucker, almost as if it were glued into place. Such superb workmanship is the essence of haute couture.

Worth had been experimenting with better fit all the time. A photograph of Marie Worth in 1864 shows her with the waistline of her dress dropped to hip level, all definition of the waistline being achieved by darting. This dress was not adopted in the 1860s but was a prototype for the 1870s. This sheath line had to be given a name so Worth called it the princess line, after the graceful Princess of Wales. It was the dominant fashion for the later 1870s and has been used time and time again since. This slim shape caused the demise of the bustle, for all styles must end once they have attained their extreme point. By degrees the bulk of the bustle was flattened and reduced until it had disappeared altogether, leaving the streamlined figure. Not since the clinging muslin frocks of the French revolutionary period had the outline of the female figure been shown so boldly. All decorative flurries were kept below the knee, occupying the hem and narrow train.

The designer must be ever alert to the exhaustion of a style, foreseeing that a fashion is becoming so established and so extreme in its development that an alternative line must be brought forth, based upon an existing trend. By 1881 Worth was of the opinion that the sheath line had been developed as far as it could go, and that it was now time for something fuller. He had not lost his fondness for the *tournure* and now proposed to do what he had done in the late 1860s, namely to start the train from the waist and cause it to fall from the back of the dress over a frame. He named this steel frame the *crinolette*, but this was misunderstood in England to mean that he was reintroducing the crinoline. *Punch* cried that Worth was responsible for bringing back that 'ancient hideous fashion' of thirty years before,[12] but it was not so. The *crinolette* was a form of bustle, squarer than its predecessor and less frivolous in its decoration. The 1880s was an earnest period full of moral concern, and the clothes reflected this spirit by being more severe. Women's wear became more tailored, more obviously masculine in style, and the hand of a master was essential if the result was not to look too stark. Many Worth gowns survive from this decade, and it is remarkable how well shaped they are without looking hard.

By this time Worth was approaching his sixtieth year, and was so famous as the great man-milliner that he was regarded as the ultimate authority in anything to do with dress. When the new Rational Dress Society in England recommended that women should wear some sort of trousers, as opposed to the restricting sheath line, there was some anxiety as to whether Worth would approve the proposal.[13] If he, as high priest of fashion, said that trousers for women were correct, then it could mean the end of the dress. But Worth was no revolutionary, nor was he a subscriber to the views first advertised by Mrs Bloomer. He did not give the suggestion his blessing, and trousers for women had to wait until the next century. Indeed even he might have found the introduction of trousers beyond his powers in 1881.

The last fashion with which Worth was concerned was the *gigot* sleeve. Historical styles of dress were a continual influence upon nineteenth-century costume design, and Worth himself built up a reference library of costume histories as well as of photographs and engravings of famous pictures. Portraits by Largillière, Nattier or Vigée-Lebrun all served for inspiration, as did portraits of the Elizabethan period. In the sixteenth century the development of the head of the sleeve as a dominant fashionable feature took place over a period of forty years from a slight puffing up of the head in the 1560s to the enormous leg o'mutton form of around 1600. The commercial nineteenth century encompassed this growth within a period of ten years. A feature such as a large sleeve can be vulgarized quite easily by

17 *Overleaf left* Race-course costumes from Maison Worth. Left, a dress of cream bengaline striped with bands of suede cloth, with a sash of green oriental silk embroidered in gold. Right, a coat of heliotrope bengaline, with a waistcoat of turquoise blue satin emerging below the waist, and a skirt of pink faille veiled in embroidered net, 1888.

18 *Overleaf right* As seen at the Louvre, a Worth coat in wool with jet bead embroidery and jet fringes. Collar and cuffs of Persian lamb, 1893.

mass producers who can produce sleeves which look like balloons. Worth treated the sleeve with far more delicacy, achieving his effects not just by padding the sleeve head but by pleating and folding the material to create size without rigid bulk. Mastery of material was again an essential component, and the fluid nature of Worth's *gigot* sleeves was an improvement upon the stiff Elizabethan originals.

Worth approached the construction of clothes from his understanding of fabrics. Having worked in textile houses for twelve years before he started making dresses, he knew the nature of each textile intimately and therefore could plan the parts of a gown to accord with the characteristics of the stuff. He ensured that the warp of the fabric always lay in the direction of the main movements of the body, so that the construction did not fight against the cloth. He often designed a dress by modelling the material upon the figure of the costumer herself, so that the fall of the fabric guided the final composition. He was not one to design a style in the abstract; it had to come from the feel of the material in the hands. The gored skirt was an improvement in construction which grew out of such experiments with fit. Hitherto, superfluous stuff at the top of the skirt panel had been crammed into the waistline, but Worth cut all this away. By making skirt panels narrow at the top and wide at the bottom, one could obtain a very neat waist while still having a voluminous hemline. Behind all Worth's fashions there lay this superb control of line. Dressmaking is, after all, a form of engineering: it is three-dimensional construction work, and Worth appreciated this better than any contemporary. By understanding the fundamental geometry of the subject he could transform dressmaking into sculpture.

In addition he was influenced by contemporary industrial practice, and adopted 'mass production' techniques into his dressmaking. With so many hundreds of ladies all wanting day costumes, dinner dresses and ball gowns all at the same time, and for each fashionable season, he had to evolve a very adaptable system. Maison Worth therefore came to operate with a range of interchangeable parts, using stock patterns of sleeve, bodice, skirt and drapery which could be combined in different compositions, like prefabricated parts. Such patterns did sturdy work, for they were used time and time again over the years. Fashions might change but the basic elements in construction did not. A bodice design of the 1870s could still be used in the 1880s by simply adding a flange to give it greater length. It was the superb shape of these basic parts which always gave Worth's fashions their perfect line. He had a filing system of the measurements and individual features of each customer from which models and gowns were made. When he died, *L'Illustration* wrote: 'We must do justice to Worth: he was the first to take female costume away from routine and bourgeois pettiness; the first to place Parisiennes upon the triumphant road of art, and to teach them not just to clothe themselves, but to adorn themselves.' For he was an artist.

3 'La Belle Époque': 1895-1914

Only nineteen years elapsed between the death of Worth and the outbreak of the First World War, which was to destroy much of the world which he had known. Throughout this period the house he had founded continued in the same grand manner as the most august establishment of its kind, but changes were taking place and his sons had to cope with them. First among the new problems was that of competition. It was inevitable that Charles Frederick Worth's success in the 1860s and afterwards should make other men and women want to emulate his example. Their efforts did not constitute a serious challenge until the 1890s when a number of couture houses were founded, which did not shake Maison Worth to its foundations but which did take away some custom and challenged its monopoly. Worth's sons responded to this challenge in different ways. Both had been working in the couture business for twenty years when their father died, so neither of them lacked experience, but they were rather opposite in character. Gaston, the elder, was the business manager, the administrator, the man who sat in committees at the Chambre Syndicale de la Couture Parisienne. Jean-Philippe was the artist, the designer, a man of some temperament, who liked to think that nothing would change and he could continue to design in the same luxurious manner as his father had done.

For much of the period he did precisely that, for there was no sudden diminution in orders for state occasions and major social events. When his father died, Jean-Philippe was already designing and making the trousseau and wedding dress for what New York society regarded as the social event of the decade, the marriage of Consuelo Vanderbilt to the Duke of Marlborough. The reluctant bride, in this union of an English title with American money, has recorded that Jean-Philippe supervised the fittings himself. There was an evening-dress of sea-blue satin, the train trimmed with white ostrich feathers, and a gown of pink velvet decorated with sables. Neither of these gowns was what the nineteen-year-old bride would have chosen for herself. They were decided for her by Jean-Philippe Worth and the duke as being suitable for a duchess. She herself would have prefered something simpler, like the white tulle dress Worth made for her coming out at a ball given by the Duc de Gramont early in 1894.[1] This is a classic illustration of a problem which Maison Worth was to face more and more in the twentieth century. The grandest orders came to it almost automatically, but the taste of young people was moving away from such splendour.

Jean-Philippe was a master of opulence. Even Poiret, who was to receive much criticism from Worth, admitted that Jean-Philippe could create gowns that were wonders of art and purity. He could make a sleeve from a tulle scarf, caught at the wrist by diamonds.[2] Worth prided himself on being a master of simplicity, but it was simplicity of the richest kind. He would design a robe of white brocaded velvet, with a statutory court train of four yards of geranium-coloured velvet lined with silver tissue and caught at the shoulder by diamond loops, for a presentation at Buckingham Palace. Or a simple shape of black net, sewn all over with black diamonds, and costing 1,000 dollars. He could not conceive of a dress that was without splendour.[3]

His father had allowed Jean-Philippe considerable freedom to design during his lifetime, but it had meant walking something of a tight-rope, for old Worth had considered innovations in dress or textiles as his own prerogative. Nevertheless Jean-Philippe had been given such opportunities as designing all the clothes for the opera singer, Nellie Melba. In 1891 he created a cloak of cloth of gold, hand-painted and sewn with jewels, for Melba to wear in *Lohengrin* during her visit to Russia. It was so lovely that even the Empress of All the Russias felt compelled to take it up and stroke it, exclaiming at such beauty. Melba was Jean-Philippe's loyal customer thereafter, repeatedly returning to Paris for collections of new clothes. It was he who taught her the importance of looking as marvellous as she sang, so that her stage presence would be as striking as her voice, and she was most grateful for the constant advice he gave her. She described Jean-Philippe as being a complete Frenchman, with polished manners and a little beard. As far as she was concerned he was a genius, who could tell what dress a woman needed after studying her for just thirty seconds. This was, of course, a skill he had learned from his father, but Melba was not to know this, for she only saw the great Charles Frederick at a distance.[4]

Another leading lady from the theatrical world was the great Italian actress, Eleonora Duse, whom Bernard Shaw considered better than Sarah Bernhardt. She came to Jean-Philippe for all her stage and personal clothes, and since she had to travel widely to perform in Europe and the Americas she considered a superb wardrobe to be essential. A slender woman with a most expressive face, her appearance in historial drama gave Jean-Philippe the opportunity to design period costume, in which he had inherited his father's interest. Accurate reconstruction had been one of Charles Frederick's principles, and his son maintained the same approach. Indeed Jean-Philippe was not adverse to dressing up himself. Masquerade parties were still highly fashionable, and he would attend costumed as a rajah or as a photographic negative. Such entertainments were still big business for Maison Worth. One of the most memorable was the masquerade given by the Duke of Devonshire in 1897 as one of the festivities during Queen Victoria's diamond jubilee celebrations. For this, Jean-Philippe dressed Mrs Henry White in a Veronese costume and Lady Randolph Churchill as a Byzantine empress. Occasionally men too would order fancy dress from Worth's. The Duke of Marlborough, for instance, ordered a Louis XV style outfit, consisting of a straw-coloured velvet suit embroidered with silver, pearls and diamonds, with a waistcoat of white and gold damask. The jewels took months to sew on, and the suit cost 5,000 francs for just one night's revelry at the Devonshire's.[5]

Expenditure at this level was nothing compared with some of the imperial

19 Charles Duke of Marlborough in the Louis XV costume created by Jean-Philippe Worth for the Devonshire House Fancy Dress Ball, 1897.

orders which Maison Worth was accustomed to receiving. Charles Frederick had dressed empresses in two coronations; in 1896 it fell to his son to design the robes for the Empress Alexandra of Russia, the last of the czarinas. He chose cloth of silver embroidered in pearls. The Empress Dowager, Marie Feodorovna, had been a customer of his father's for many years, so the new head of Worth's had to design for her too, which meant that nearly all the ladies at the Russian court had to have Worth dresses as well.

This pattern was repeated with the British Empire. Charles Frederick Worth had dressed a vicereine of India, Lady Lytton, in the 1870s; consequently the vicereine in 1903, the Marchioness of Curzon, went to Jean-Philippe for her dress for the Delhi coronation durbar. He made her a gown which was to become known as 'the peacock dress', for it was embroidered all over with a pattern of peacock feathers in a metal thread. The eye of the feather was formed by sewing a hard Indian beetle's wing-case at the centre, in glossy green. The bodice was decorated with loops of diamanté and gilt, and the neckline was trimmed with tulle. All round the hem of the dress ran a froth of white roses. Here again his father's influence can be discerned, for old Worth had created a peacock masquerade gown for the Princesse de Sagan back in the 1860s.

Such patronage continued well into the new century. Even in 1914, on the very eve of the Great War, Jean-Philippe Worth could rattle off the tastes of his royal clients. Queen Elena of Italy liked soft blue-greys, Queen Wilhelmina of Holland preferred tailor-made gowns, the Dowager Queen of Spain was fond of bright fabrics such as patterned brocades, but Alexandra of Russia was not very interested in clothes so he usually designed simple dresses for her.

House policy under Jean-Philippe remained exactly the same as that laid down by Charles Frederick. A woman must be guided in her desire for a new fashion. It was the couturier who could best judge what colour and style of dress would best suit a client's individual qualities. She should leave everything to him in the secure knowledge that his decision would supply the perfect answer. Yet no woman should be a slave to fashion. Let her retain what was good if it suited her, rather than aping every variation in the mode regardless of whether it flattered her or not. Let her select a classic line, because that would last her better than any seasonal frivolity. As an example he suggested the princess line which his father had invented. Jean-Philippe was still making dresses to this design; there had been variations in its application, but the basic concept still held good. 'It was beautiful in its inception,' he said, 'and remains beautiful today.' For him fashion should be evolution and never revolution.

His brother Gaston, the business manager, saw that the political situation in the new century was by no means stable. Competition between the German and the British Empires was increasing, and one could not guarantee that all the royal courts of Europe would last for ever. Already one of their father's most beautiful patrons, the Empress Elizabeth of Austria-Hungary, had been assassinated by an anarchist in 1898. Gaston realized that the commercial existence of Maison Worth in the future could well

depend on its attracting a much broader, and less royal, custom.

Jean-Philippe did not agree, and he felt no taste for designing simpler, cheaper clothes. As an experiment he reluctantly agreed to his brother's engaging a young designer. The young man selected, named Paul Poiret, had been trained at one of the new rival houses, Maison Doucet, and he was to work at Maison Worth from 1901 to 1903. Gaston Worth explained the situation to him. Worth's had the most elevated and richest clientele and it clothed all the courts of the world, but the pace of life was changing, and even princesses occasionally travelled on buses or walked down the street. They did not need magnificent robes so often. 'We are in the position of a great restaurant, where one would prefer to serve nothing but truffles. We therefore need to open a counter for fried potatoes.'[6] It was Poiret's job to supply these chips, by designing simple, more practical clothes.

His efforts did not meet with success. When he showed one of his designs to Jean-Philippe, the great man went pale. 'You call that a gown? It's a dishcloth!' Worse was to follow. One day when Jean-Philippe was keeping his eye on the rue de la Paix, on the lookout for arriving customers, he spotted the Russian Princess Bariatinsky. The salon was tidied, the *vendeuses* (saleswomen) lined up, and Worth greeted the princess as she emerged from the lift. She was short and all in black, smoking a cigar, a very forthright and independent old woman. Poiret unwisely showed the princess one of his creations. It was a very plain robe, a kimono of black cloth trimmed with black satin, hardly the sort of thing to show to an elderly lady who was long accustomed to splendid attire. The princess exclaimed that it was horrible, and rather like one of the sacks the Russians used to put the heads of decapitated criminals into. Jean-Philippe was furious at such a *faux-pas*, and Poiret's career at Maison Worth was brought to an abrupt end.

That may have stopped the introduction of radically simpler clothes at Maison Worth for the time being, but outside tastes were changing and Worth's would have to accommodate them sooner or later. Jean-Philippe remained as designer until 1910, but then after thirty-six years in the business he decided to lighten his load by restricting himself to grand commissions and engaging a junior designer to do the routine work. The Worths prided themselves upon being a dynasty of designers, Jean-Philippe having maintained his father's prestigious creation, so it was from among the family that an heir was sought. Jean-Philippe had a daughter, Andrée, who in a very appropriate union of haute couture and jewellery, had married Louis Cartier. She was now a young mother, so the solution had to be found from among Gaston's offspring. He had two sons who were now both introduced into the business. The elder, Jean-Charles, was to be the junior designer, while Jacques, who had read medicine, was to take over some of the administrative and managerial work from his father. This was the structure of the house until the Great War.

The principal challenge to this noble establishment was to come from a woman, Mme Paquin. Charles Frederick Worth might have driven female dressmakers into the shade in 1860, but by the end of the nineteenth century they had learned their lesson and were setting up business in the same pattern. Mme Paquin, as she was always known, founded her house in 1891,

46

having been trained as a dressmaker at Maison Rouff. She had the great advantage of being married to a banker and businessman, Isidore Paquin, so she had no problems over raising money or managing a firm, and her husband helped her to build a flourishing business. When he died she ran it single-handed for a time, but then called in her brother, Henri Joire, to take over the management, leaving her free to concentrate on design.

In tastes, Mme Paquin was not far removed from Jean-Philippe Worth, for she loved to create opulent, luxurious clothes. She became noted for her superb lingerie and her richly romantic evening wear. It was the glamour of her dresses, as opposed to the dignity of Worth's which most appealed to the contemporary press and to her customers. A review of her presentation at the Brussels Exhibition of 1910 typified their reaction to her designs. 'The surety of Mme Paquin's taste is once again revealed by a splendid group of some twenty mannequins in evening gowns of a richness and elegance to dream on, which compose a very artistic ensemble, of an incomparable harmony of nuances.'[7] *Le Gaulois* reported that her clothes display was a fairyland. She possessed a talent for the subtle blending of materials and colour tones, and this was ideally suited to the new taste for pastel tones which came into fashion in the early 1900s. Pale pink, lilac, grey and blue, allowed her to create gowns of misty beauty from chiffon and silk.

Mme Paquin was a shrewd judge of which styles would appeal to the majority of women. She knew that violent changes of fashion were not appreciated by any except the young, so the development of her dresses was gradual. When she made an innovation it was for very practical reasons. In January 1913, for example, she produced a dress which was intended to solve one of the problems of modern living. As many ladies had duties or even jobs during the daytime, and had to rush off to functions in the evening without having time to go home and change, she designed a dress that was a blend of tailoring and drapery. It was smart enough for a daytime function, yet soft enough for informal evening occasions. In April 1914 she considered the slit skirts that were then high fashion, to be too immodest for they displayed the leg. She therefore experimented with cut until she produced a pattern which still looked narrow but which allowed for easy walking without revealing the leg. Like the creations of some other women couturiers we shall encounter, her fashions were far more sensible than some of the things dreamed up for women by men. She wore her own designs, and consequently she knew whether they were practical or not and where any problems might arise. She became known in Paris as a woman of great elegance, and this reputation was based upon her own study of the workings of dress.

Mme Paquin prospered so well that by February 1913 her directors were able to pay a dividend of 9 per cent on top of an interim dividend of 5 per cent, giving a total of 14 per cent for the previous year.[8] In January 1913 she was awarded the *Légion d'Honneur*, the first woman dressmaker to be so honoured. The press hailed her as the queen of Paris fashion. Her establishment at 3 rue de la Paix was next door but two to Maison Worth itself, and in her outside workrooms she employed a thousand people. Worth had opened a London branch for the greater convenience of the

21 *Overleaf left* Dress and jacket by Madame Paquin for a garden party, the hem of the skirt heavy with embroidery, 1901.

22 *Overleaf right* Paquin afternoon gown, decorated with broderie anglaise, 1901.

British aristocracy at 3 Hanover Square, so Mme Paquin opened one at 39 Dover Street, which engaged three hundred workers during the season. With an eye on American millionaires, she had a branch in Buenos Aires, and a fur house which was run in conjunction with her brother as Paquin Joire, at 398 Fifth Avenue, New York.

While it was Poiret who started taking models on foreign tours, Mme Paquin, being a shrewd businesswoman, was not slow to follow suit. She sent her sister-in-law, Mme Joire, on a tour of the United States with four mannequins to show her dresses. The team visited Philadelphia, Boston, Pittsburgh, Chicago and New York. At first 3 dollars were charged for tickets, but demand was so great that the price was raised to 5 dollars in an effort to reduce interest but still requests poured in. Crowds had to be turned away. Couture was moving into a new era where the public wanted to see what hitherto only the richest customers could see. Similarly in 1913 Paquin tango dresses were displayed in a tango fashion show at the Palace Theatre, London. The *Daily Express* commented that 'these new fashion shows were rivalling in popularity the ordinary theatre play'. As it happened Mme Paquin's relation with the theatre was quite close, for she made clothes which were designed by Paul Iribe in 1910 and by Leon Bakst in 1913, and when Bakst tried his hand at designing townswear she made them up too. The actress Gaby Delys, who made no secret of her rich lovers, was her most glamorous customer, not to say the most notorious.

If Maison Worth dressed royalty and opera stars, and Paquin dressed high society and entertainers, there was still room for other couturiers to clothe the newly rich. Three women founded and ran the house of Callot Soeurs. The daughters of a Parisian antique dealer who made a speciality of old fabrics and lace, they were to use these fabrics as the basis of their designs. The principal designer of the three was Mme Gerber, with Mme Vertran as second designer. During the *belle époque* their house was in the rue Taitbout, not far from the Paris Opéra, although they were to move to the avenue Matignon in 1919. Their most important customer was Mrs Rita de Acosta Lydig of the United States who made her money by marrying an elderly millionaire and divorcing him four years later. He gave her an enormous settlement, which enabled her to embark on a life of extravagant pleasure. The tastes of Callot Soeurs and Mrs de Acosta Lydig were very closely matched, favouring a highly individual way of dressing: old velvet and old lace for ornate day dresses, heavy satin for evening. Clothes in the 1900s were becoming simpler, but Callot Soeurs continued to make heavily decorated gowns, overhung with networks of beads or tiers of lace. In this they satisfied their main customer so well that she was their principal source of revenue – until she went bankrupt in the 1920s.[9]

The house of Jacques Doucet was very different from Callot Soeurs. He was literally born in the very centre of haute couture, for his birth took place in February 1853 at 21 rue de la Paix, over the luxury lingerie shop which his grandmother had founded. When a young man Doucet inherited this shop and set about converting it into a couture house. He loved elegance and beauty, and was eager to acquire a sophisticated appreciation of the arts and to lead the life of a gentleman. There was something of a dichotomy in his

character in that he adored dressing women and making them beautiful, but at the same time he was unhappy about being in trade and wished to be known as a collector and patron of art.[10]

None of the couturiers at the turn of the century wished to shock their customers. Beautiful clothes superbly made, in the tradition of Charles Frederick Worth, were still the essence of haute couture. Doucet fitted into this pattern and made a great success of it, his insistence upon excellent workmanship earning him a name for quality. Ladies patronized his house for this very reason. They wished to look luxuriously dressed, but to have had very conspicuous clothes would have been considered bad taste. A courtesan might order something very striking, but a lady had to be more reserved. Her clothes could be rich, but restrained. There Doucet excelled, with his fondness for blending colours and his feeling for iridescent silks.

Due to his success and financial gain Doucet was able to realize and satisfy his artistic yearnings. Influenced by the taste of the Goncourt circle, he built up a collection of eighteenth-century works of art which he housed in his *hôtel* at rue Spontini, where he gave elegant parties. When that collection was as complete as he wanted it, he started building up a library of art and archaeology, which he was to present to the University of Paris in 1919. Such an interest in the arts was not unprecedented in couture, for Worth had used the paintings of the seventeenth and eighteenth century as a constant source of inspiration for costume design. While the successful couturier would certainly commission portraits of himself from a contemporary artist, it was unusual for a couturier to set himself up as a leading collector of fine art at that time. Worth had been content to succumb to the 1870s and 1880s mania for collecting old china, of which he amassed some 25,000 pieces. Doucet went beyond this, in the belief that the status of patron and collector would grant him an *entrée* as an equal to the highest circles in society. Whereas Worth had elevated the status of the couturier, Doucet wanted to be a gentleman despite being a couturier.

When Doucet died in 1929 his establishment was merged with that of Doeuillet. This firm was founded in 1900, but it was not one of the greatest houses, and it was given less coverage than its rivals by such magazines of the early 1900s as *Les Modes*. As one of the backers of the *Gazette du Bon Ton* it made regular appearances in that magazine, with fairly simple clothes typical of the 1910s. By 1923 the fashionable press was criticizing Doeuillet for the confusion of its offerings, and as it had no clear-cut style to offer, it failed to attract customers and so declined. It was possible for a couture house to manage without lavish press coverage but it was not easy to do so. Drécoll opened in 1905 and lasted until 1930. Its promenade gowns and evening dresses were shown in *Les Modes*, but on the whole its designs were a lot fussier than those from other couture houses and it did not become a major establishment.

Another of these relatively short-lived houses which survived for about a generation was that of Chéruit. Most of the advertisements for Chéruit from 1907 to 1914 show walking suits and afternoon dresses, outnumbering evening wear, which suggests that the house concentrated on day clothes rather than on gala gowns. The house was run by Mme Chéruit, and when

24 Callot Soeurs' principal means of financial support, Mrs Rita de Acosta Lydig.

25 *Overleaf left* A Doucet teagown modelled by the actress Réjane, who wore his clothes to great effect on stage and in society, 1902.

26 *Overleaf right* Doucet dinner gown of Venetian lace typical of his restrained luxury, 1903.

53

27 *Above* Mlle Harlay in a Doeuillet afternoon gown, edged with lace frills, 1904.

28 *Right* Promenade gown by Drécoll, trimmed on the bodice and hem with spotted net, 1905.

29 Chéruit promenade suit,
with long sleeved waistcoat.
The skirt is semi-draped.
Drawing by Pierre Brissaud,
April 1913.

ZUT!. IL PLEUT!!...

Petite robe de promenade de Cheruit

the First World War started she was one of the few couturiers to mount an
autumn collection, saying that women had to have clothes whether there was
a war or not, and that dressmakers had to continue to earn their living.

Chéruit continued into the twenties. When the premières of the cinema
had become as important as those of the theatre, Chéruit was one of the
couturiers to introduce cinema capes in 1923. The house showed dresses
hand-painted with Cubist decoration in 1925, but it was not always so up-
to-date with contemporary taste. Its evening skirts of 1924 were fuller than
the lean line then in fashion, and its love of ornamentation and embroidery

appeared increasingly excessive as taste moved towards a more sophisticated simplicity. The fashion press stopped regarding the house as important enough to include in its reports from Paris, and so Chéruit faded from the scene. It is imperative than any couture house wishing to survive longer than the life of its first owner or designer, should recruit new talent which can respond to changes in taste. When it fails to do so, its clothes become increasingly conservative, and its appeal is restricted to an ageing and diminishing clientele.

An interesting development in the late nineteenth and early twentieth centuries was the entry of two English tailoring firms into the sphere of French female couture. As observed in chapter 1, tailors had continued to make women's riding habits despite the advent of dressmakers. A classic example of this tradition can be seen in the tailor Henry Creed. He came from a long line of men's tailors in London and had his premises at 33 Conduit Street. It was Creed who made the clothes for that leading dandy, the Comte d'Orsay, which led to him receiving orders from other French noblemen as well as from the English. From the 1840s he was making suits for Albert the Prince Consort, and was appointed as the maker of riding habits to Queen Victoria and the princesses. Prince Albert recommended Creed to Napoleon III, which led to Creed opening a tailor's shop in Paris, first at 59 rue Neuve and later at 25 rue de la Paix. There he made English suits for Frenchmen, and riding habits for French women, including the Empress Eugénie, and became something of a cross-Channel commuter as a result.

At the fall of the Second Empire, Creed rushed to Paris to save his business. He was severely wounded during the Paris Commune uprising of 1871, but survived and managed to rebuild his business and to hand it on to his son. This was another Henry Creed, born in 1863, who expanded the firm and became tailor to the monarchs of Austria, Italy, Russia and Spain. He used to travel from court to court with a team of twenty hands, suiting his royal clients on their own premises. It was the Duke of Alba in Spain who told Henry Creed to expand into female tailoring. Creed had made the duke a tweed suit which the duke liked so much that he said that Creed would have to make one in the same tweed for the duchess, otherwise she would be outshone. The appearance of the duke and duchess in matching suits started a minor vogue, and other ladies began asking Creed to make their town suits. Thus from around 1905 Creed became a ladies' tailor as well as being a gentleman's tailor. In addition to the suits for kings and emperors, he was now making suits for the Queen of Italy, the Infanta of Spain and the Grand Duchess Vladimir, and for stage queens such as Mary Garden, Réjane, and Gaby Delys, and the mysterious Mata Hari, who had the good sense to face the firing squad in her Creed suit.[11]

The house of Redfern began differently but ended up with a similar status. John Redfern started in a small way as a draper at 41 High Street, Cowes, on the Isle of Wight, in the 1850s. By 1871 he had expanded his business by becoming a silk mercer and a maker of mourning wear as well. Then Cowes became the centre of the yachting world, for the rich were taking to yacht racing in a big way. Redfern flourished under such

30 John Redfern's trousseau for Princess Beatrice in light wools; far left, travelling gown, yachting or tennis suit, walking habit, and dress, 1885.

31 Mary Garden in Redfern's town dress of pleated Rajah silk, with matching cape and lace blouse, 1905.

customers, and rapidly adapted to suit their needs. All the ladies arriving at Cowes for the racing and the messing about in boats needed yachting outfits, so Redfern developed his mourning dressmaking line into a ladies' tailoring department. His tailored yachting suits were so successful that Redfern opened a London branch at 26a Conduit Street. His sons joined the firm and it became known as Redfern & Sons, with the ladies' tailoring house in London, and the Cowes establishment expanding into three shops, selling silks, linen, dresses, shawls, mantles and millinery. The year 1879 was an important one for John Redfern, for a suit he made in jersey wool was worn by Lillie Langtry, the Jersey Lily herself, which made the outfit immensely popular. Business flourished and his clientele was drawn from the higher social levels. In 1885 Redfern was commissioned to provide the travelling suit, yachting suit, riding habit and some dresses for the trousseau of Princess Beatrice. By 1888 he was able to style himself 'Redfern & Sons, ladies' tailors by appointment to Her Majesty the Queen and H.R.H. the Princess of Wales'. The success of his tailored wear encouraged increasing demands for fashionable clothes, so Redfern moved into couture dresses. The establishment as ladies' tailor now occupied 26 and 27 Conduit Street and he opened a separate dressmaking house at 27 Bond Street for couture clothes.

Redfern's creations were being illustrated by *Harper's Bazar* in the United States, so to satisfy American customers he opened branches in New

York and Chicago. France did not ignore this new house, and prospects there seemed so favourable that Redfern opened a couture house in Paris itself, before Creed did so. In the space of thirty years he had progressed from draper, to ladies' tailor, to couturier. When he died his business was so widespread that no one person could direct it single-handed. His son Ernest took over the English and American sections, and Charles Poynter was appointed head of the Paris house. The creations at Maison Redfern became a regular feature of fashion magazines by the turn of the century, and the house gained full French recognition by being made a member of the Chambre Syndicale de la Haute Couture. Its elegant suits and gowns gained it a wide custom, one of its most famous customers being the Scottish opera-singer, Mary Garden of the Opéra-Comique, who was celebrated for her interpretation of the leading female role in Debussy's only opera, *Pelléas et Mélisande*. Maison Redfern was never one to lag behind when change was in the air, and in 1908 it was one of the first houses to present the Grecian line, with its higher waist and fillet-bound hairstyles. The Princess of Wales retained her liking for Redfern's clothes, and when she became Queen Alexandra the house was granted her royal appointment, following the natural ending of Queen Victoria's.

The *belle époque* ended with Worth and Paquin as the dominant houses, and with Creed and Redfern occupying a respectable second rank and continuing longer than Chéruit or Doeuillet.

4 The Revolt against Fashion

The excesses of fashion have been criticized down the ages by both Church and State, but it was the very changeability of fashion which has most worried artists. In particular it presented a problem to portrait painters, for their sitters would often insist upon being portrayed in the height of contemporary fashion. This might seem splendid at the time, but thirty years later those styles would be very much out of fashion, and quite ridiculous in the eyes of a later generation. What could infuriate an artist more than that his picture might seem out-of-date, merely because the sitter's clothes had dated? Consequently there have been periods when artists attempted to get round this problem. In the second half of the seventeenth century they painted ladies in their nightgowns and shifts, in the hope that, since the styles of nightgowns changed very little, they would look classical.[1] Similarly in the eighteenth century Sir Joshua Reynolds persuaded his lady clients to give up their hoops and be painted in narrower, more classical clothes, for the sake of art. This striving after classical eternity was adopted by the world of fashion itself at the end of that century, when to look as antique as a Roman or Greek became the vogue, so the problem subsided as far as artists were concerned. But by the 1820s and 1830s fashion was shedding the classic look in favour of a Romantic mixture of the lace collars of the 1630s and the full sleeves and ringlets of the 1660s, and the difficulty reappeared.

This time the reaction was rather different. A group of English painters, the Pre-Raphaelites, created a non-fashionable costume for the women in their circle and used it in their pictures. They did not attempt to persuade lady sitters in general to adopt this costume, for with the exception of Millais they were not society portraitists. Strangely enough, however, men and women who admired Pre-Raphaelite works adopted an unusual form of dress in order to show their artistic solidarity with the avant-garde. This did not happen in France; the French Impressionists in their revolt against academic standards did not dress their wives in unfashionable costumes, nor did their supporters attempt to display their opinion by inventing a uniform for that purpose. But the English are always prepared to be unconventional in their private lives while remaining quite conservative in their politics; in France the opposite is perhaps true. From England the influence of the Pre-Raphaelite dress spread to the United States and Europe, and in the end it came to affect fashion design in Paris itself.

Criticism of fashion in the nineteenth century came from two quarters, from the medical profession as well as from artistic circles. Over the years some of these arguments merged, and a critic of dress might use both lines of reasoning in the same essay. What angered doctors most was the increasing tendency towards ever smaller waists as dictated by Paris. In 1851 one medical practitioner, Lionel Beale, published a general medical work in which he devoted a section to the iniquities of corsets, pointing to the deformation of the internal organs which they imposed. The tight lacing to which females were subjected from childhood caused their bodies to grow into unnatural shapes and destroyed the support from the muscles and the spine. The liver and kidneys were displaced and the lungs compressed. He earnestly hoped that 'the time will arrive when stays will be considered antiquities of the mediaeval age, and be only preserved as relics to adorn the museums and halls of the curious'.[2]

Such views were supported by the art historian, Mrs Merrifield, in her *Dress as a Fine Art* of 1854.[3] Corsets, in her opinion, were the cause of the frequency of miscarriages and of the birth of deformed children. She recommended that tailors and dressmakers should be made to attend schools of design and to learn the true proportions of the human figure, so that they might create clothes appropriate to the natural shape. She particularly censured Paris fashion magazines such as *Le Moniteur de la Mode* and the fashion illustrators such as Jules David and Réville for publishing exaggerated drawings of the latest styles. Foolish women attempted to impose these extravagant fantasies upon their own bodies, in the fond belief that there were fashionable ladies in Paris who really looked like that. Such misleading drawings should be stopped, she argued, and more realistic illustration be introduced.

The corset industry did attempt to counter such attacks. The anatomical corset maker, Mme Roxey Caplin, of 58 Berners Street, whose adaptors had won a prize at the Great Exhibition of 1851, published a reply in 1856. She insisted that the correct corset, of the sort which she sold, designed according to the age of the wearer, was the best remedy. She claimed that her corsets allowed for proper breathing and gave the sort of support which the body itself could not provide.[4]

At this time there came from the United States an attack upon the whole structure of female fashion as it existed in the 1850s, expressed by a movement known as Bloomerism, although Mrs Bloomer herself did not actually start it. Amelia Bloomer was born in 1818 in New York State, and after a short career as teacher and governess married Dexter Bloomer in 1840. He was proprietor and editor of a weekly journal, *The Seneca County Courier*, and in 1849 Mrs Bloomer was drawn into journalism through her work for the temperance movement. Since that was run mainly by men, she founded a small paper, *The Lily*, as a voice for women in that crusade. One of her contributors was a Mrs Elizabeth Stanton who was an advocate of female rights. Mrs Bloomer came to agree with many of Mrs Stanton's views, and from 1850 her little paper bore the legend, 'devoted to the interests of women'. In 1851, possibly to be provocative, her husband's paper published an article suggesting that the short skirts and ankle-length trousers worn by Turkish women were far more practical than the voluminous, long skirts and petticoats of European and American women. Mrs Bloomer took up the challenge in *The Lily*, and agreed that this completely different costume for women would be very sensible. She was not the first person to adopt the new dress; Mrs Stanton's cousin wore it for about three months, and then Mrs Stanton herself, before Mrs Bloomer took the plunge. The New York press latched on to the story and turned it into a sensation – women in trousers! Demand for *The Lily* soared, and requests for patterns poured in from American women, while Mrs Bloomer as editor of the women's paper was seen as the prophet of a new concept of clothing. She was invited to go on lecture tours, and went wearing the new costume, finding it most convenient for travel, although the subjects she spoke on were not dress but temperance and women's suffrage.[5]

The news crossed the Atlantic very quickly, and *Punch* and the London music-halls had a field day, ridiculing the costume and asserting that women were now trying to take over the established role of men. This, of course, was not true. Mrs Bloomer simply wanted votes for women and a more practical costume, and not the total reversal of social roles. Some Englishwomen were sympathetic. Mrs Merrifield wrote that Mrs Bloomer's costume was more modest and convenient than anything else being worn by women at the time.

The dress was in fact a compromise between fashionable taste and practical needs. It followed the fashionable line in having a fitted bodice, although not fiercely corseted, and it kept the fullness of skirts. The most radical change came at the knee; the skirt stopped at this point and revealed full trousers *à la Turque* which clothed the legs from waist to ankle, where they were gathered in. No part of the legs themselves was revealed, and there was less chance of an ankle being exposed than by the raising of a conventional skirt. Nevertheless, the very suggestion of women wearing anything resembling trousers was anathema to Western man. The majority of women themselves were amused by the suggestion, but they were too conditioned by conventional views to dare to do anything 'indelicate' or 'too forward'. By the end of the 1850s Mrs Bloomer decided to give up her reformed costume. It was not the failure of the idea which worried her, but the publicity and the sensationalism with which it had been treated by the press. She feared that this outcry was diverting serious attention away from a far more important question: that of women's rights.

It was against this background of debate over feminine attire that the Pre-Raphaelites began working. The brotherhood had been founded in 1848, the leading members being Millais, Holman Hunt and D.G. Rossetti. They were opposed to the empty theatricality of much contemporary painting, and sought to create an art which projected ideas while remaining scrupulously faithful to reality. In this quest for truth, as they saw it, one of the matters to which they had to give their attention was costume. Any artist dealing with a subject involving clothed characters has to see the costumes in front of him if he is to depict the folds and drapery convincingly. The diary of Rossetti's teacher, Ford Madox Brown, is very informative on this point. In 1847, when he was preparing to paint his picture of *Whycliffe reading his translation of the Bible to John of Gaunt, Chaucer and Gower*, he had to obtain medieval costumes, so he went down the Strand and to Holborn looking for suitable materials. He bought ten yards of flannel, some plaids, some cotton velvet, some genuine velvet, and some yellow brocade. Ermine he hired.

BLOOMERIANA. A DREAM.

He then cut out and made some of the costumes himself and hired a sewing woman to make the rest.[6] The Pre-Raphaelites were no different. When Holman Hunt painted *Valentine rescuing Sylvia from Proteus* in 1851, he made two of the costumes himself and did some of the embroidery[7], and it was he who designed the wedding dress for young Ellen Terry in 1864 when she married the painter G.F. Watts. There was nothing conventional about it, for he had it made of brown silk to show off her tawny hair, and gave it very full sleeves of a Renaissance kind. Watts later painted her in the dress.

Rossetti was particularly interested in medieval themes, so some knowledge and recreation of the clothes of that period was necessary. He was fortunate in that his model and later his wife, Elizabeth Siddal, was a seamstress. Not only could she make clothes for his early pictures, but she could also make her own clothes for everyday use. It was probably Rossetti who encouraged her to give up conventional fashion, and the dresses she was to wear were probably a joint creation of his ideas and her ability. The result was very original. In 1854 Rossetti drew several studies of Elizabeth in one of these dresses, not all in the privacy of the studio, but when staying at Hastings. They show her in a very simple dress with no corset and no crinoline, at the very moment when small waists and enormous crinolines were the height of fashion. The bodice is especially interesting as it is a loosely fitted wrap-over type, so very unlike the tight contemporary ones. It is a very easy and undemanding costume, in contrast to all the difficulties of management and breathing imposed by crinolines and corsets. It was a costume to relax into, which one could not do in a modish creation.

Rossetti and Elizabeth Siddal did not devise this form of dress with the intention of converting womankind. They were not dress reformers with a crusade to pursue. The costume was made for their own purposes, so that Rossetti could study how a draped skirt fell, and appreciate the qualities of cloth hanging in a way similar to that worn in the Middle Ages. This was something he could not see in fashionable skirts, where the fabric was stretched out over the wide frames of crinolines. Nevertheless this form of costume was adopted by some of the other ladies in their circle of friends. Effie Ruskin, wife of the famous critic who so championed Pre-Raphaelitism, wore it herself when on holiday in the Highlands.[8] Eleven years later photographs of Mrs Jane Morris show her in a similar dress.

This group is interesting as all the photographs were posed by Rossetti

33 The artistic person should avoid fashionable dress in a portrait: G.F. Watts, 'Ellen Terry'.

34 Elizabeth Siddal, drawn
by D.G. Rossetti in the very
simple clothes he advocated
for artistic purposes.

himself, and show the sort of costume effects he was looking for in order to
use later in his paintings. Jane Morris's dress is not exactly the same as
Elizabeth Siddal's, as it is much looser, falling from the shoulder into a wide
sack. It could be worn with a belt so that it formed deep folds, or without a
belt so that it formed a great sweep of fabric. It also has a train. Other
elements, however, are very similar – notably a pleated bodice and loose
sleeves, although Jane's are longer and they have cuffs. By this date, 1865,
Rossetti's women friends had been wearing this form of costume for eleven
years, and later photographs of Mrs Morris show her still wearing such
garments in the 1870s. She did not ignore fashion completely, for she wore
her waists fairly high and put her hair up when it became stylish to do so in
the 1870s. Nevertheless here was a form of dressing, distinctly different
from that dictated by Paris, which had become established within an artistic
circle.

During this period criticism of fashionable dress had not ceased. A strong
attack was published by John Leighton in 1870 in a social essay against the
horrors imposed by fashion on the natural body of woman.[9] He illustrated
the displacement of the spine, the distortion of the organs, and demanded
the total abolition of corsets. He placed some hope in the fact that some
women were now being allowed to receive higher education. Could they not
set an example and enlighten their less fortunate sisters, he asked. Over the
years some of them did, partly through artistic dress and partly through

rational dress. Artistic dress began to flourish in the 1870s. Rossetti was seen as the prophet of much that was advanced in taste, with his fondness for medieval subjects, his early collecting of blue and white china, and his admiration of Botticelli. So the clothes of the women in his circle came to be adopted by other women who wished to appear as members of the same sophisticated set.

It was not completely unprecedented for ladies with artistic tastes to dress differently from less 'enlightened' sisters. The Pattle sisters of Little Holland House were known in London in 1849 for their unusual clothes which they designed themselves with ample folds and long cloaks.[10] What was different about the 1870s was that the adoption of artistic dress was not confined to the artistic circles around individual painters, but became a vogue followed by women from a wider background.

The aims of Pre-Raphaelite dress, as it became known, were laid down very clearly in 1879 by one of its advocates, Mrs Haweis. The shape of the dress itself should not contradict the natural shape of the body. Thus corsets and any other form of tightness were to be avoided. A natural waist, an easy skirt, high-cut sleeves allowing for arm movement, and a flowing train, were the aim. There were no rigid rules, however, regarding details: necklines could be whatever pattern the wearer fancied, sleeves could be copied from any number of paintings by Van Dyck, Rubens or Rembrandt. Colour was important, however. Strong aniline dyes had been used in high fashion since the mid-1850s, but aesthetes found them far too garish. Avoid such startling colours, said Mrs Haweis.

But when you see a colour which is moderately dull in tone, and so far indescribable that you question whether it is blue or green, green or brown, red or yellow, grapple it to your soul with hooks of steel: it is an artistic colour, and will mix with almost any other artistic colour. No artistic colours are unduly bright.[11]

Such subdued colouring became a common feature of artistic dress. It was not admired by everyone; Vernon Lee went to a party given by a painter and described it as being 'full of weird people, women in cotton frocks of faded hues.' But demand for such stuffs was sufficient for some shops to specialize in them. The most celebrated emporium to do so was Liberty's in Regent Street, whose 'art colour' silks became big business.

Typical of the sort of woman who went in for artistic dress was Mrs J. Comyns Carr, wife of the director of the new Grosvenor Gallery, which was founded in 1877 as an alternative exhibition centre for contemporary painters who were *persona non grata* at the Royal Academy. Vernon Lee called her 'the artistic siren' of the day, and when George du Maurier created his character, Mrs Cimabue Brown, as The Aesthetic Woman for his cartoons in *Punch*, Mrs J. Comyns Carr liked to think that he had based the character upon herself. She created some of her clothes herself. In 1883 she made a white muslin dress which she boiled in a potato steamer to produce a crinkled effect. When Ellen Terry saw this dress she liked it so much that she asked for a copy of it for her next theatrical role, and appointed Mrs Comyns Carr as her theatre costume designer.[12] By this time artistic dress was often being called aesthetic dress.

36 Artistic dress as adopted
by sophisticated society.
J.A.M. Whistler, 'Symphony
in flesh colour and pink: Mrs
F.R. Leyland', 1873.

AN IMPARTIAL STATEMENT IN BLACK AND WHITE.

ÆSTHETIC LADY AND WOMAN OF FASHION. | WOMAN OF FASHION AND ÆSTHETIC LADY.

37 The looseness of aesthetic dress as compared to the tightness of fashionable dress. George du Maurier: 'An Impartial Statement in Black and White', 1881.

Du Maurier's cartoons in *Punch* were just one of the sources of criticism of the aesthetic movement, but he was unbiased enough to admit that some women looked better in artistic dress than they did in the height of fashion.[13] Not so the old painter, Frith, who thought aesthetic dress to be so eccentric compared with the beauties of contemporary fashion. He determined to show the contrast in a painting, because by 1881, wearers of artistic dress could even be found at a private view at the Royal Academy.[14] The Pre-Raphaelite mode was finding its way into the very best circles! In the event, Frith's painting was by no means as damning as he intended. The fashionable ladies sitting in the centre are fiercely corseted from bust to hip, and have such narrow skirts that walking and climbing stairs must have been far from easy. By contrast, the artistically clothed ladies look comfortable in their easy-fitting garments. It is true that many wearers of such dress were artistic snobs and social climbers, but not all. Serious thought had been given to freeing women from the tyranny of fashion, and artistic costume was one result.

A different approach came from those who thought healthy dress was more important than beauty. The Rational Dress Society was founded in June 1881, with Viscountess Haberton as president. She was an admirer of

Mrs Bloomer's costume of thirty years before, and considered some form of trouser-skirt for women to be just as sensible for her day as it was for Mrs Bloomer's. She started wearing a divided skirt which was named the Haberton, and sometimes Turkish trousers. Not every member of the movement followed her example. Ada Baillie of the National Health Society thought that Bloomerism had been, and still was, too violent a change for women. She felt that the princess gown was the best solution, for being cut in one, it avoided any need for tightness at the waist, and the weight of the skirt was supported by the bodice.[15] Both women, however, subscribed to the basic views of the Rational Dress Society, which were that any attempt by high fashion to impose unhealthy and unnatural garments upon women was to be resisted, and that any form of dress which restricted the limbs, prevented exercise and deformed the body was an abomination.

Ada Baillie said that corsets should only be worn for remedial effects, and recommended that fat women should try the boneless stays invented by two undergraduates at the new women's colleges of Newnham and Girton and sold by the Rational Dress Society. These reformed stays were shown at the Hygienic Wearing Apparel Exhibition in 1882. In 1883 a joint exhibition was mounted by the Rational Dress Society and the National Health Society, and in 1884 they participated in the International Health Exhibition at the Royal Albert Hall. The clothes they showed were of a practical nature, and strongly reflected the increasing amount of sporting activity being undertaken by women. Walking, climbing, cycling, tennis,

38 W.P. Frith, 'The Private View at the Royal Academy'. Aesthetic dress worn by the two women on the left, and the woman with the train next to Oscar Wilde, among the fiercely corseted ladies of fashion.

roller-skating, cricket, riding, and yachting were being pursued by younger women, and sometimes were included in their education. As we have seen, Maison Redfern waxed rich on this expanding need for sporting clothes. A divergence came into being at this time between townswear and country wear; the former could remain as ornate as fashion desired, but the latter became as practical as the rationalists required. Dress reform succeeded, but only in the sphere of feminine activity where greater mobility was essential. Much thought was given, for instance, to devising a sensible skirt for cycling which did not get caught in the chain or wheels. Ada Baillie strongly recommended her tailor, Mr Goodman of Albemarle Street, as a specialist in cycling clothes. By the 1890s the needs of the bicycle had brought about a revolution that had been debated on and off for over forty years. Girls started wearing bloomers on bikes, that is, a knee-length version like breeches. Sport had achieved what example and argument had not.

The 1880s saw the entry of specialized clothes into a woman's wardrobe. It was no longer a case of day dresses and evening gowns with the odd riding habit; the younger woman now added clothes for half a dozen sports or hobbies. So far so good, but this still left high fashion free to be as impractical as it liked. The criticism therefore continued. In 1883 the painter Watts wrote his essay 'On Taste in Dress'. Once again corsets were denounced and the changeability of style condemned: 'What we may certainly lament is the apparent want of any principle in the fluctuations of fashion, excess in one direction being invariably followed by excess in the opposite direction.'[16] The small waist was a deformation. Watts insisted that the natural proportions of classical Greek art should be the ideal. Venus de Milo was beautiful without stays. Not for him the medieval lines of artistic dress – costume should be Grecian.

This was very much in tune with the current trend in painting. In addition to Watts himself, Lord Leighton, Albert Joseph Moore, Sir Edward Poynter and Sir Lawrence Alma-Tadema were all painting classical Greek subjects. Strangely enough, Oscar Wilde, the leading example of an aesthete and a member of the Rational Dress Society, shared the view that Grecian art, combined with principles of health, was the source from which future costume should come.[17] In 1890 when the Rational Dress Society's journal had ceased to exist, a new dress reform group was established to publish sound ideas on costume. This was the Healthy and Artistic Dress Union, and Watts and Sir Arthur Blomfield were two artists among its vice-presidents. The Union advocated classical dress, and examples of suitable designs were drawn by Walter Crane for its journal *Aglaia* in 1894. This sort of reformed dress ousted any remnants of pseudo-medieval artistic dress. Henceforth artistic dress had to be Greek.

By this time dress reform was no longer simply an English and American concern. The Germans had long been concerned with healthy costume, particularly Dr Jaeger with his sanitary woollens. Belgium expressed interest, in the person of Henry van de Velde. When this rebel against corrupt official art married in 1894 he not only designed his house as an example of pure style, but also the furnishings, crockery, textiles, and, as the *coup de grâce*, artistic dresses for his wife, so that the whole ensemble,

40 Paris makes a gesture towards aesthetic dress, the tea gown, by Worth, in a caftan of beige coloured cloth over a dress of stamped velvet in maroon. Revers of white plush, 1891.

including the inhabitants, was an artistic whole. In 1896 he again designed artistic dresses which had high waists in the classical manner, although occasionally he used a waistless design with Watteau pleats in the back.[18] Such clothes were included by the German, Heinrich Pudor, in his *Die Frauenreformkleidung* of 1903. Let German women cast off their stays and go Grecian! was his message. Pudor suggested high-waisted or waistless dresses which, to cope with the northern climate, could be made of wool and have long sleeves. Such clothes were certainly sensible, for the fashionable waistline of 1900 was even smaller than that of the 1880s. It deserved to be resisted, and paintings by such continental artists as Peter Kroyer and Eugen Spiro show some women doing so. In Munich, *Simplicissimus* even had cartoons on the rejection of the mode. The revolt against fashion might only be manifested amongst artistic and intellectual groups, but it could be seen from Scandinavia to the United States.

And just how much attention to all this criticism did the world of haute couture condescend to pay? Slowly, little by little, it did respond. It had to yield an inch if it wanted to retain a yard. The abolition of corsets was a suggestion it resisted until the twentieth century, but from the 1880s one relaxation was allowed. Tea parties were of course long established social occasions, particularly among ladies. When several ladies were staying at a house party, they did not have to dress up to go out to tea but could relax indoors and take tea together. Such informal gatherings could allow for less formal clothing. Paris responded with tea gowns – waisted or loose gowns in soft fabrics, a lighter and more fanciful version of the dressing gown. Ladies did not discard their corsets when wearing tea gowns but they could slacken the laces and relax for an hour or two before donning their fiercely boned dinner dresses or evening gowns.

If Paris was reluctant to abandon corsets, it showed no hesitation in adopting aethetic dress. Maison Worth itself created artistic dresses, for did not Charles Frederick Worth consider himself an artist? Certainly he would respond to any proposals made by the world of art, providing they were not revolutionary, such as abandoning stays. Given his fondness for historical costume, artistic dress gave him an opportunity to play with such features as Watteau pleats and Renaissance sleeves, so he did not hesitate. His grandest customers allowed themselves to be dressed as Monsieur Worth thought right, so one finds the Duchess de la Torre wearing artistic dress and having her portrait painted in it by de Beers. Princess Viggo had a Worth artistic gown, now in the Brooklyn Museum, in which the Renaissance influence is very strong in the sleeves, billowing sweeps of ice-blue silk bedecked with satin bows down the seam, but the waistline is very high in the manner of the First Empire. Such mixing of historical elements was characteristic of artistic dress wherever it occurred. Jean-Philippe Worth also designed artistic gowns. Indeed he said that they had a dateless quality which made them highly appropriate for portraits. He made such gowns for ladies going to be painted by Dagnan-Boureret,[19] so here were a couturier and a portrait painter displaying the same concern over the problem of pictures being dated by the costumes in them, as artists in the seventeenth and eighteenth centuries.

41 What Worth approves,
the aristocracy must follow –
the Duchess de la Torre in a
Worth artistic dress, portrait
by de Beers.

Fashion was not slow to accommodate the neo-classical look either. As
early as 1881 *Harper's Bazar* in the United States was illustrating Grecian
aesthetic dresses (designer unnamed), available either with the high waist or
in contemporary corseted versions. An archaeological effect was added by
the reproduction of gold jewellery which had been excavated by Professor
Heinrich Schliemann; 'Grecian' in this case being wide enough to include
Etruscan and Trojan artifacts. Interest in aesthetic dress was sufficiently
strong in Paris for Liberty's to open a Paris branch in 1890, after selling
several aesthetic creations at the Exposition Universelle the year before.[20]
Thus a viable market existed there for such clothes, below the level of haute
couture.

Where sportswear was concerned, the fashion houses had to supply what
their customers wanted. When the clients changed their habits, no couturier
could ignore the fact and survive. As seen with Redfern, the vogue for sports
was becoming so popular that it could make a sportswear shop rich enough
to become a couture house. Such healthy pastimes were started by the
wealthy. The bicycle became fashionable while it was an expensive

innovation; high society took to it because no one else could compete, but once bicycles went into mass production the rich turned their fancy to something else. Yachting was one area where only the very wealthy could play. Emperors and kings had their yachts, so of course Maison Worth made elegant yachting outfits for the royal ladies to wear. Shooting was another royal pastime, so the couturier made shooting suits for the ladies. Whatever the game, once the rich played it, their clothiers would create the apparel for it.

The introduction of teagowns, artistic dresses and sportswear shows the world of high fashion reacting to specialized activities. It could embrace these innovations and use them to help maintain its prestigious position. Yet where it resisted change most strongly was in the one area where criticism was sharpest, that of fashion itself. There it would allow no compromise of its freedom to introduce such styles as it pleased. A pioneering attack against corsets had appeared as early as 1829 by Dr Andrew Coombe; it was eighty one years before the most avant-garde couturier dared to dispense with tiny waistlines. The call for Grecian proportions had been heard since the late

42 Two Grecian aesthetic dresses, that on the left in white silk cut on the ancient model, the second adapted to the corseted figure with pale blue cashmere body and white cashmere train, the Greek key pattern embroidered in gold. On the right an Early English dress for mediaevalists in brick red satin, 1881.

1870s, but it was not until 1908 that fashion went some way towards this ideal by reviving the empire line. As *Harper's Bazar* observed in 1894, Paris was 'the stronghold of conventional dress'.

In being so slow to change, haute couture merely reflected the nature of its clientele. The designer might be free to introduce an innovation in a fashionable line, but he was not at liberty to present his customers with changes which would have shocked them. To do so would have been economic suicide. Couture dressed the most aristocratic and the most wealthy classes, both of which were very conservative entities. Their new clients, the North and South American *nouveaux riches*, in their eagerness to rise in society wanted exactly the same clothes as the lords and ladies. None of these groups wanted radical change in their wardrobes. The tastes in fashion reflected the styles of living. So long as ladies did not work, spent the day on social visits, dined out and went to balls, fashion clothed them in non-functional gowns. Only when ladies abandoned these activities could fashion do so. In other words, the social pattern had to change before couture could. True the clever couturier would be alive to the whispers of change and launch fashions to suit them, but he would fall flat on his face if he dared to be outrageously ahead of current mood. Moreover youth was not yet in fashion. Most of a couturier's customers were married women who had been wearing corsets all their lives. Only when these ladies were ready for a revolution in dress would it be time to launch one.[21]

5 The Poiret Revolution

Into the haughty, elegant world of haute couture there dropped, in the first decade of this century, an outrage by the name of Paul Poiret. Paris was confronted by a designer who treated fashion as if he were a showman, who shouted his wares like a circus ringmaster, and who liked to shock. The rejected junior designer at Maison Worth set himself up as a professional couturier. Fashion would not be the same again.

Paul Poiret was born in Paris in April 1879, the son of a draper. His early years were to be dogged by his father's lack of understanding of the young Poiret's artistic instincts. As far as Monsieur Poiret was concerned, the best thing for young Paul was to train for the trade, but the youth proved to have other interests. He would frequent the Comédie Française to see Bernhardt and Réjane perform, and he would sketch their costumes. He would haunt the Louvre, fascinated by the pictures of Nattier, Vernet, Ingres and later Botticelli, drawing what he saw. In 1896 he passed his baccalaureate in letters and sciences and would have liked to have gone to university, but his father would not hear of it. Business was what the father understood, and it was there that he expected his son to earn his living. He placed the seventeen-year-old Paul as an assistant in a friend's umbrella shop. Young Poiret did not like this at all, but he was under age, and he had no money of his own. He could not be master of his affairs until he was twenty-one, and even then his choice would depend on his resources.

After the tedium of umbrellas all day long, Poiret would amuse himself in the evening by modelling muslin dresses on a 40-centimetre figure, aided by his three sisters. He started designing dresses in sketchbooks and one day he decided to take some of these designs along to a couture house, which was a very daring thing to do. He called on Mme Chéruit, and to his delight she not only bought twelve drawings at 20 francs each, but told him to come back with more. After that Poiret made a point of visiting couture houses when he was out delivering umbrellas, dropping in at Worth, Redfern, Doucet, Rouff and Paquin, to offer a few designs. When Poiret was nineteen, Jacques Doucet who was always one to encourage young talent, suggested that he might like to come to work for him. This was what Poiret wanted, but his father had to be dragged along to Doucet's office before he would believe the news and give his consent.

Doucet had no faith in soft treatment for novices, and flung Poiret into the busy world of the workrooms as assistant to the tailor. Here he learned the professional way to make clothes, how to cut and how to drape. He was allowed to continue with his ideas for designs, and his first design Doucet had made up, a short cape of red cloth, sold no less than four hundred copies. Knowing of Poiret's love of the theatre, Doucet allowed him to create a robe for one of his most famous customers, Réjane. She wanted a voluptuous mantle for a role as a café concert star, and young Poiret devised a wrap of black taffeta, hand-painted with mauve and white irises and covered with black tulle. Pleased with this, Doucet in 1900 allowed Poiret to dress Sarah Bernhardt when she was to act the title role in Rostand's *L'Aiglon*, although the young man infuriated the temperamental actress by sitting in at her rehearsals, which she did not allow.

It was obvious that Poiret had ability, but what he lacked was personal style. Doucet told him to acquire more savoir-faire, go to premières, visit smart hotels, and make himself known outside the couture house. Poiret took his advice, buying himself his first smart English suit, from Hammond's in the Place Vendôme, just a few steps from the rue de la Paix. The social education of this budding man-about-town was unexpectedly advanced when a wealthy American actress took a fancy to him. They embarked on a six-month affair, during which time Poiret was taken to smart resorts, luxury hotels and fashionable restaurants, experiencing as much high life as he could have wished. This idyll ended when Doucet found out that Poiret was designing clothes for this woman, who then had them made up by her own dressmaker. As Poiret was still employed by Doucet, his designs belonged to that couture house. Doucet was so annoyed he fired Poiret on the spot.

Poiret was now twenty-one and eligible for his military service. As he had educational qualifications he was only required to serve for ten months, unlike others less fortunate who had to do three years. Back in Paris in 1901 Poiret looked for work and, as we have seen already, was engaged by Gaston Worth. That was a disaster, and in 1903 Poiret was out of work again. He was full of ideas and he had acquired expensive tastes, but he did not seem able to avoid upsetting his employers. Therefore he decided to become his own employer and start his own couture house. He was twenty-four when Maison Poiret opened its doors in a shop at 5 rue Auber. It had a staff of eight seamstresses and a capital of 50,000 francs. Its greatest need, in a city full of couture houses, was to attract attention. Poiret made passers-by notice the shop by putting on dazzling window displays, which in Paris were and still are a recognized art. He matched his displays to the seasons, using fiery fabrics for autumn, softer tones for summer. Intrigued by these, some ladies dropped in. To lend Poiret a helping hand, the kindly Doucet persuaded Réjane to call. She did so, liked what she saw, and started placing orders for dresses. With this fashionable star as his advertisement, Poiret's business got off to a good start.

By 1905 Poiret was successful enough to marry. His bride was nineteen-year-old Denise Boulet, the daughter of a textile manufacturer, and just as Charles Frederick Worth's career had changed when he married and started making clothes for his wife, so now Poiret's career took on a new dimension from the personality and physique of his wife. Denise Poiret was slender and quite unlike the fashionable figure of the day, the big-busted mature woman, with generous curves in front and rear, attired in sweeping trumpet-shaped skirts and elaborately laced blouses, and unswept hair topped by large confections of feathers or flowers. A slender young thing simply had no place in such a scene. But fashions can be made to change, and with his wife as his new ideal woman, Poiret began to design clothes that would best suit her. He knew something of art history and had admired the works of David and Ingres, so he was aware that there had been a vogue for slender women in the early days of the nineteenth century. He knew that the high-waisted empire line of the period was very flattering to thin women with small busts. Could he not therefore apply the same principles to a slender woman in the early days of the twentieth century?

The first barrier to any such development was the corset, the S-shaped construction which forced figures to be projected up in front and down at the back. When first launched, this form of corset had been regarded as more natural than the previous in-and-out shape of the 1890s, but it was still too extreme for Poiret's purpose. Later, Poiret claimed in his autobiography that he abolished the corset.[1] This was not true, for what he really did was to alter the shape of it. To achieve an empire line one abolishes tight waistlines. This was where Poiret brought greatest relief for the much abused female figure, by removing constriction in the middle. But a slender line still needed to be controlled, and prominent hips and bottoms were not to be liberated in the same way as the waist. On the contrary, Poiret extended the corset to the top of the thighs. His ideal woman had no hips or buttocks at all! As Watts had complained, fashion swung from one extreme to another.

When a man is a pioneer is it is not always true that he is working in an area completely untouched by his contemporaries. The feeling for liberating the body had long been expressed by dress reformers. As we have seen, they were advocating the classical high waist back in the 1880s and were still doing so in the early 1900s. Another couturier, Madeleine Vionnet, then working at Doucet's, has claimed that she persuaded the house models to give up corsets in 1907.[2] In a completely different sphere but also in 1907, the American dancer, Isadora Duncan, was performing on the Paris stage wearing no more than a short classical tunic, with no corset and no stockings either. Clearly there was a wisp of the abandonment of restraint seeping through the air, and what Poiret did was to capture it and apply it to his sphere of fashion.

1908 was the year when Poiret really forged ahead. He rented new premises, an empty *hôtel* in the Faubourg St Honoré which had a large garden where fashion parades and parties could be presented. He launched his empire line with all the publicity he could muster. He took the unprecedented step of publishing some of his designs in a de luxe booklet, engaging the young artist, Paul Iribe, for the plates. Entitled *Les Robes de Paul Poiret* and with ten illustrations, the publication sold in a limited edition of two hundred and fifty copies at 40 francs each. Not only was the idea completely novel, but the presentation was totally unlike contemporary fashion drawing. Iribe's plates were designed with great simplicity. There were no swirling figures, no elaborate backgrounds. The women are shown as static, upright, and very young. The dresses are presented in all their simplicity with great clarity, showing the very plain concept of Poiret's new line. High waists, slim figures and narrow dresses with very little decoration replace the overblown beauties of Edwardian taste.

43 The new long, lean corset frees the waist but enslaves the hips, 1908.

IN "DECORATING CLEMENTINE." ACT II.

44 *Left* The Neo-Classicism of Poiret's lean line, emphasised by Romney's portrait of Lady Hamilton in the background, 1908.

45 *Right* The lean line spreads abroad, and is here worn by the American actress Hattie Williams in *Decorating Clementine*, 1910.

The new line had to have a name, and it was dubbed *le vague* because to contemporary eyes it looked loose in comparison with the tight waists of the period. Journals such as *L'Art et la Mode* published their own drawings of the new shape, and this carried Poiret's name abroad. Lady Diana Cooper remembered looking at exmples of *le vague* in that magazine when she was fourteen, as her mother the Duchess of Rutland took it for the fashion news.[3] Poiret's new line, which was swiftly copied by other houses, received the sort of sensational publicity that other couturiers shied away from. The last thing Worth or Paquin would have dreamed of was to abandon dignity and shout one's wares in the popular press. As Jean-Philippe Worth had said back in 1903, he thought that young Poiret lowered the tone of couture. Knowing of his displeasure, American *Vogue* approached Worth for his opinion of these startling new dresses, and Jean-Philippe exclaimed that they were positively barbaric.

1909 was the year when the arrival of the Ballets Russes hit the Paris theatre and Parisian society with the impact of a psychological bomb. It was a burst of fireworks, an explosion of brilliant colour and torrid tones into a world accustomed to subdued shades and understated clothing. The sets and costumes of Bakst burned with fiery light, dazzling oranges, brilliant blues, strident greens, and spewed exotic treasures before the astounded audience. Suddenly the barbaric East was in fashion.

Poiret always claimed that he himself had set the vogue for exotic colour and oriental costumes before Bakst's designs became all the rage in Paris. This was true. He had already made a kimono when he was at Worth's, and included another in *Les Robes de Paul Poiret* in 1908. But interest in the exotic East had preceded both Poiret and Bakst. Fashions for oriental objects had been coming in and going out ever since the sixteenth century when Jesuit missionaries had started sending artifacts back to their headquarters in Rome. The seventeenth century had seen the growth of East India companies in England, France and the Netherlands, which brought in goods from the other side of the world. The eighteenth century had produced the craze for chinoiserie, while the mid-nineteenth century witnessed the outbreak of a cult for Japanese art. It was in 1858 that Japan had signed trade treaties with Western states, and the importation of Japanese art was now on a regular basis. Artists in London and then in Paris became collectors of Japanese prints, fans, porcelain and even clothing. In 1863/4 Whistler painted his *Rose and Silver: La Princesse du Pays de la Porcelaine*, a study of a girl in Japanese kimonos, and also in 1864 his *Purple and Rose: The Lange Lizjen of the Six Marks*, in which the sitter wears Chinese dress. Such subjects became favoured by painters and in 1896 for example, Wilson Steer painted *The Japanese Gown.* Thus the East had been in vogue for some time, particularly where décor was concerned. What Poiret did was to bring this interest into fashionable clothes. The impact of Bakst's stage costumes was, however, extremely important in giving this movement a brilliant showcase and in kindling a new fire within an existing fascination. In particular he gave it a new twist by awakening delight in old Russian and Tartar themes.

It should also be noted that the artistic movement known as Fauvism had exhibited its works with its violent use of colour at the Salon d'Automne of 1905. Matisse, Rouault and Dérain were among the first, to be joined later by Dufy and Braque, in rejecting academic good taste in favour of distortion, flat shapes and raw colour. Here then was another influence to suggest to Poiret that he might introduce some of its qualities into fashionable dress. This is not to deny his claim to originality. He was the first couturier to do so, but no one person can claim to have originated all the aspects of a far-reaching movement.

Poiret revelled in the oriental look, which allowed for the expression of flamboyance and luxury in dress. He illustrated the result in another booklet in 1911, *Les Choses de Paul Poiret* which had plates by another young artist, Georges Lepape from the Ecole des Beaux Arts. He had trained under that influential teacher, F.P. Corman, who could number Toulouse-Lautrec, Van Gogh and Matisse among his pupils. Lepape shared Poiret's fervour,

46 *Left* Poiret's gown 'Strozzi', with a two-tier tunic edged at the hems with brilliants; turban bound with lamé held by a buckle. Photo by Edward Steichen, April 1911.

47 *Right* Poiret's gown 'Enfer', cut all in one, the waist defined by beading, the only seams being down the sides and at the shoulders. Worn with a mantle in satin with contrasting sleeves. Photo by Edward Steichen, April 1911.

and the illustrations are full of bejewelled turbans and bead-trimmed tunics worn with slave bangles and harem slippers. Poiret further advertised his designs in this style by engaging the important art photographer Edward Steichen to record a group of his dresses for *Art et Décoration*. The models were posed casually with none of the self-conscious formality usual in fashion photography at that date. Black and white photographs could not, however, rival Lepape's lively use of colour, but they showed how the bold and young should look.

They strove to do so. To the younger person these bright colours and exotic clothes were a relief from the overladen dresses of the early 1900s. The stuffy old order was being out-dazzled, out-run and overthrown. Wearing brilliant new clothes was one way of showing the change. Some people even went so far as to wear Eastern costume proper. Lady Ottoline Morrell recorded that the wife of the painter Neville Lytton was wearing 'gorgeous Arabian dresses' in 1909, and she herself had a collection of Persian, Turkish and other oriental

48 Denise Poiret dressed by her husband for his 'Thousand and Two Nights' Persian party in 1911, with pantaloons of white chiffon over ochre chiffon, and a wired tunic in gold cloth with a gold fringe; chiffon bodice and sleeves; turban of gold cloth wrapped round with chiffon, the large aigrette held in place by a large turquoise.

49 From fancy dress into fashion – Poiret used the wired tunic for evening dress, with a white tunic, edged with black fur, worn over a black velvet skirt, lined with white silk. Drawing by Georges Lepape, January 1914.

LE COLLIER NOUVEAU
Robe du soir de Paul Poiret

garments for her guests to wear on her Thursday at-homes in 1914. As her guests included Duncan Grant, Walter Sickert, Augustus John, Henry Lamb, Bertrand Russell, Vernon Lee, Lytton Strachey, Robert Trevelyan and Arnold Bennet, it is clear that dressing up was popular among our leading artists and writers.[4]

Fancy dress parties were no novelty; indeed they were one of the regular features of high society. Poiret embarked on his own variation of dressing up by throwing wildly exotic parties at his *hôtel*. The first was a Louis XIV extravaganza, but in 1911 he epitomized the exotic fashion with his

THE NEW SKIRT AND THE POETRY OF MOTION.

Edith (breaking into a hop). "HURRY UP, MABEL; YOU'LL NEVER CATCH THE TRAIN IF YOU KEEP ON TRYING TO RUN."

'Thousand and Two Nights' party, where all the guests had to be dressed as Persians. Poiret himself appeared in a turban, while he dressed Mme Poiret in a gold tunic and chiffon pantaloons. Her tunic was wired around the hem so that it stood out all round, and over the next few years Poiret repeated this feature as part of fashionable dress for evening. Gold and silver lamé, brocade, damask and satin were all called upon for this Persian spectacular, and illustrated Poiret's wild extravagance.

Now that he was a big name in the fashion world, an innate arrogance in Poiret came to the fore. With money at his fingertips he became rude and domineering. It was goodbye to the gentleman couturier such as Jean-Philippe Worth or Jacques Doucet, to the silk top hat, the frock-coat and striped trousers which Poiret himself had worn when working for those gentlemen. Instead he sported casual suits, and dashed about in a sports car. His innovations made headlines, so he could afford to scorn the opinion of the old guard, which in its turn regarded him with shocked outrage. Jean-Philippe had a word for Poiret, and that word was 'vulgar'.

In 1910 Poiret launched a fashion which caused an outcry of a kind that no couturier before would have contemplated. Having liberated the waistline in his slim *vague* look, he developed this slimness to its ultimate

50 The problems of Poiret's hobble skirt, with narrowness taken to an impossible extreme. 'The New Skirt and the Poetry of Motion', 1910.

extent. He refined it to the 'logical' ideal, by making it as narrow as could be. He created the hobble skirt, a garment so narrow that walking was almost impossible. For a woman to move without splitting the material her legs had to be shackled by tapes, so that she could only take tiny steps. He who had freed women from one unnatural imposition now introduced another. The howl of protest which broke out in the international press was un-precedented. When Charles Frederick Worth had abolished the crinoline it had caused a sensation in the world of fashion, but it was not a matter upon which newspapers would publish critical leaders, or which would incite readers to write in protest against, for it was eminently sensible. Poiret's hobble skirts were a different matter altogether. They were so manifestly impractical that persons outside the sphere of fashion could plainly see the folly. Criticism poured in from all directions, and from Rome there came papal condemnation.

The sensation was, of course, good publicity. Poiret was now the evil genius of high fashion, who expected women to hop instead of walk when he snapped his fingers. It was the sort of publicity that the other couture houses did not want, but it catapulted Poiret's name across Europe and the United States. There was such excitement about the hobble skirt that women took to it in large numbers, although certain modifications had to be made. Discreet pleats at the side, or a concealed slit, were essential for the skirt to be worn at all. Nevertheless the narrow line was firmly in fashion; in the space of three years Poiret had banished the swirling trumpet skirt from the fashion stage.

Poiret was now notorious, a universal talking-point, with the result that foreigners wanted to see the man and his clothes. An invitation came from Berlin, so Poiret set out in two cars with his wife, his mannequins, a collection of dresses and even a film of his models. This was a completely new departure. No couturier before Poiret ever set out with a travelling fashion-show-cum-lecture-tour in order to promote his creations. Such blatant commercialism was beneath their dignity. If a lady wanted their clothes let her come to Paris to be fitted, for did not all the best people come to Paris? But here was this fellow, Poiret, taking dresses round European capitals like a travelling salesman! Such considerations did not bother Poiret. Berlin, Vienna, Brussels, Moscow and St Petersburg were all visited in 1912, and wherever he went he drew the crowds. Normally haute couture clothes were only seen on their wealthy wearers or in copied versions in expensive shops, but here was a parade of the originals with a commentary from their creator. Naturally fashionable women rushed to see it, and were wildly enthusiastic. Orders poured in and the money rolled.

During this period Poiret had caused an even greater scandal. He so liked the harem trousers that he had designed for his wife at their Persian party that he tried to launch trousers for women as fashionable dress. Let there be trousers for daytime and trousers for evening, slim pantaloons worn beneath knee-length tunics. Although women were now wearing bloomers for cycling, the suggestion that trousers should form part of their normal wardrobe was greeted with furious condemnation. This time Poiret had gone too far. All the censure that had fallen on Mrs Bloomer in the 1850s was now matched by the storm that descended upon Poiret. Female suffrage had become very much a political issue by this time. Some American women had the vote already but in other countries the argument still went on, with occasional violence. Poiret's putting women into trousers touched a rare nerve where men were concerned. It suggested that women really were attempting to seize the masculine role. They damned it from all sides, and no husband would have allowed his wife to adopt such a costume. It would take a world war to alter the attitude towards the idea of women in trousers. But Poiret was a prophet, for trousers did come, and sooner than most people imagined.

None of this sensation detracted from Poiret's fame. In 1913 he went another step beyond his contemporary couturiers by embarking for New York with a collection of his clothes. The Poiret circus was visiting the United States. Priests thundered from their pulpits and moralists set up an outcry that Poiret's fashions were a manifestation of evil, coming to pollute the pure American ways; all of which was of course very useful publicity for Poiret. The reaction he encountered in the United States was more extreme than the one he had received back home in Europe. It ranged from outright damnation from the Bible belt, through accusations that some of his fashions were in breach of the sumptuary legislation of some of the states, to rapturous adulation from the women of fashion.[5]

What affected Poiret most on his American visit was the discovery that department stores in New York and elsewhere were selling unlicensed copies of his dresses and using his name without having sought his permission. The protection of copyright was the thorny problem of haute couture and almost impossible to police properly, for merely by changing a detail or two a copier could claim that his dress was a different design altogether. The infuriated Poiret, as soon as he was back in Paris, tried to organize better protection for original designs. He asked Philippe Ortiz of *Vogue* to undertake the necessary consultations with the other couture houses. This led to the creation in 1914 of Le Syndicat de Défense de la Grande Couture Française, with Jacques Worth as vice-president and the support of Paquin, Chéruit, Callot Soeurs and the textile manufacturers, Rodier and Bianchini.[6] Poiret himself was the president of the association.

The outbreak of the First World War soon put such schemes in the shade. Several couture houses announced that they would not present any collections that summer. All male couturiers of suitable age were called up. In August 1914 Poiret was ordered into the French infantry. Jacques and Jean-Charles Worth were soon in khaki, and Doeuillet joined the volunteers. Couture was left in the hands of the old designers and the ladies.

Poiret had a useless time, engaged in trying to invent a military uniform which used less material than the current model. As soon as peace was made he flung himself back into couture, and his first collection in 1919 was as exotic and flamboyant as his pre-war presentations. Some of his designs were used very successfully by the theatre, but the vogue for oriental fantasy was in decline. Some of it survived in the cinema, notably in *The Sheik*, presenting that new phenomenon the film star, in the person of Rudolph Valentino. Mrs Valentino became a customer of Poiret's, but in the main,

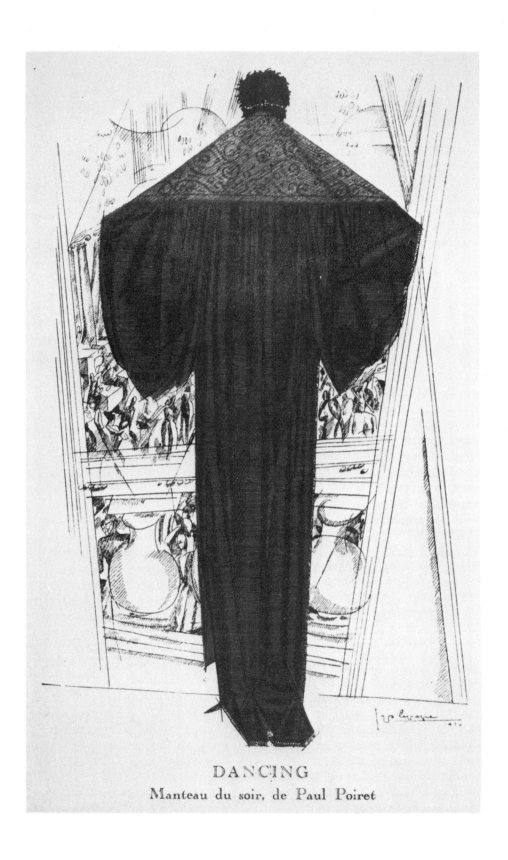

DANCING
Manteau du soir, de Paul Poiret

such exotica were fading out from the sphere of fashion. The post-war period was to be very different from the years preceding it.

From then on Poiret's story is one of decline. He was a one-man show, no founder of a dynasty of designers, and when that man's talent was slipping his couture house was in trouble. The truth was that he had outlived his usefulness as far as fashion was concerned. His ideas had set the mood for six years before the war, but times were changing. Some industrialists had become richer, but many members of the aristocracy found their incomes falling, while others had been driven out of their countries. Not everyone could afford to be as extravagant as they were before the war. There was relief that the war was over, but there was a growing desire that the society which had led to the worst war in modern history, was not to be imitated. The young were looking for a brave new world and to the wonders of science, and turning their backs on the pre-war period. Flamboyant dress was on the way out and much simpler clothes were coming in. Turbans, hobble skirts and wired tunics were *passé*.

Poiret's tragedy was that he could not adapt. He made a second trip to the United States in an attempt to boost sales, but his clothes were considered too fussy. He was unable to simplify a dress enough; he could not resist adding decoration and piling on the ornaments, at a time when the vogue was for stripping clothes clean. The fashion press stopped reporting his collections; public interest was over. To reorganize his affairs Poiret formed himself into a stock company, only to find that the directors severely curtailed his extravagant notions. His debts mounted and in 1925 he was forced to sell his collection of contemporary árt, but things still got worse. In 1929 his directors closed the company down; his wife sought a divorce; all his possessions were sold. In the general economic gloom of that year, no one wanted to know about Poiret. Left to himself Poiret wrote his autobiography.

In 1933 the store of Printemps offered him a good opportunity to design clothes for the mass market, but he upset the firm with his irresponsible attitude towards money. He did not understand the meaning of self-discipline and economy. His troubles deepened, and in 1937 the question was raised at the Chambre Syndicale de la Haute Couture whether the industry should grant Poiret a pension. The suggestion was vetoed by Jacques Worth. It was not their duty to support an ex-couturier, who should have attended to such matters himself. Poiret drifted away from Paris, took up painting and had some bit-parts in French films. Friends gave what help they could during the German occupation, but he died in those grey days of 1944, aged sixty-five.

What did such a man achieve? Undoubtedly he was a liberator. His lean line was the death knell of the tightly restricted waist. Years were to pass before women abandoned the corset altogether, and girdles are still in use today, but the end had come to tiny waists. No longer were women laced up from cradle to grave. For the first time in all the years of debate about dress reform, fashion itself moved away from the waistline. There were to be a couple of attempts to bring back small waists, in 1939 and again in 1947, but these were not permanent impositions, for the crucial period is in girlhood.

51 Poiret's evening mantle 'Dancing', falling from a shoulder piece of rich brocade. Drawing by Lepape, March 1920.

93

The growing body has to be encased and the internal organs forced downwards to achieve a really small waist in adulthood, and girls are no longer treated in that way.

A second freedom introduced by Poiret was the reduction in the number of clothes worn by women. His narrow styles did not need layers of petticoats, so the legs were no longer impeded by a clutter of chiffon and silk. With his clothes one petticoat was enough, instead of a dozen. The reduction in numbers had the additional benefit of lightening the load. A woollen dress of 1900, with several petticoats underneath and a heavily boned corset, was pounds heavier than a simple Poiret dress with just one petticoat and his longer corset. The days when clothes were an actual impediment were passing. From then on, whatever the fashionable variations, clothing was to be lighter, easier, less restricting. The heavily laden woman was being replaced by a more streamlined sister, who did not need a carriage to transport her from one shop to the next. The female body has managed to move in some astonishing creations, but its task is greatly aided by the clothes being lighter.

Poiret was the second couturier to stress that fashion was part of the applied arts and not just a frivolous subject unworthy of serious consideration; but whereas Worth had been content to call himself an artist, Poiret set about founding an art school. Impressed by the developments he had seen in contemporary art while on tours of Austria, Belgium and Germany, such as the paintings of Gustav Klimt and the architecture of Josef Hoffmann, Poiret decided to encourage such trends in the field of textile design. He founded a school of decorative arts called Martine, after one of his daughters, but instead of taking mature students or trained designers, he recruited girls with no previous art training. With no teachers to impose ideas or restraints, he encouraged the girls to draw and paint plants and flowers as they saw them in their own untutored way. He then took some of these simple designs and used them in textiles and carpets, which caused some excitement in artistic circles, for they could be compared to the 'primitive' effects being sought by the Fauves. One painter in particular became interested, and that was Raoul Dufy, who also contributed designs for textiles which Poiret had printed. The striking effects Dufy created with bold, crude designs impressed even the textile industry. Poiret had helped Dufy by giving him work when his painting was proving very unremunerative, but the textile business recognized a strong talent when it saw one, and in 1912 Dufy was snapped up by the firm of Bianchini-Férier. Paul Iribe was also engaged by Bianchini, so two Poiret protégés found themselves designing for a wider, commercial market. Such losses did not undermine the success of Martine. The girls proved so prolific that the studio was made into a firm of decorators, undertaking the furnishing of a whole house from curtains, carpets, screens, wallpaper, to chairs and tables. Here again Poiret was a pioneer, for no couturier before had attempted such a formal entry into that field.

Lastly, Poiret was the first couturier to give lectures on his subject. The Worths and Mme Paquin expressed their opinions in interviews, but they did not travel around Europe and the United States talking to audiences.

52 Poiret, right, supervising a fitting with his tailor M. Christian, c. 1924, marking with chalk where an adjustment was needed. Scalloping the front of the coat was the sort of decoration he could not avoid. His working jacket would not have been approved of by the senior generation of couturiers who wore morning coats.

Rober pour l'été 1920.

53 Raoul Dufy: summer frocks in fabrics from Bianchini-Ferier, with abstract patterns gaining dominance, May 1920.

Accordingly Poiret's views are of some importance. Whilst he was hailed and fêted on his first American visit as the king of fashion, it was a title which he insisted was very misleading. The successful couturier was not a despot or dictator who changed clothes, altered necklines or reshaped sleeves simply because he felt like doing so when he woke up in the morning. On the contrary, the couturier was a servant who had to be on the constant look-out for the earliest signs of a change in his mistress's attitude. He was a slave who needed very sensitive antennae to discern when a woman's interest in a fashion was beginning to tire. Thus the couturier does not change a mode out of caprice, but because he feels that his clients themselves are changing. Moreover the changes in fashion were part of an evolution, not a sudden jumping to and fro between extremes for the sake of novelty.

He said that it did not take a genius to detect that fashion would change, but he was annoyed at the way in which manufacturers blamed him for the alterations. When hats were lavishly decorated, Poiret had observed that one day plain hats would come into vogue, for it was inevitable that there would be a reaction against excessive ornamentation sooner or later. The producers of hat trimmings were most disturbed and begged him not to discourage

I Worth's invention of the princess gown was immediately copied by other dressmakers. On the left is a princess gown ball dress in green crêpe de Chine trimmed with lace and bunches of anemones. Right, a ball dress in coral pink taffeta, with tulle fichu draped *à la paysanne*, and trimmed on the corsage and skirt with embroidery and pink begonias. 1878.

2 Visiting ensemble consisting of tunic and skirt with train, for
the lady who had to walk only from her carriage to the front
door. On the right, a short costume for a teenager in peacock
blue foulard. Tunic and pleated skirt trimmed with embroidery.
Boy's suit in grey wool with velvet waistcoat. 1879.

3 Paquin's town dress for summer 1910, original design from the couture house's own design department, full of the hauteur of the clientele.

4 What to wear on the promenade at Nice, summer *toilette de ville* designed by Francis. c. 1912.

5 *Toilette de bal* showing the Greek look that was in fashion and which owed more to the Napoleonic Empire's vision of ancient Greece than to the classical period itself. Designed by Laferrière who had been important dressmakers in the 1850s with court patronage, but who were ousted from the front rank by Worth. c. 1912.

6 Three Empire day dresses with Poiret's use of much stronger colour as opposed to the pastel shades of his contemporaries. c. 1912.

7 Afternoon gown by Jeanne Lanvin with transparent cape. Girl's dress decorated with embroidery. 1922.

8 Evening mantle by Paul Poiret for the *femme fatale* of 1922.

their trade, but, Poiret insisted, such a command was completely outside his power. He could not prevent a change in taste.

Poiret was also displeased with American buyers, who only purchased the obvious and banal models which would sell most, and ignored more artistic designs. Such commercialism was not to his liking. What was more, he found American women very imitative in their dressing. The United States was far richer than France, yet American women did not express their individual personalities in their clothes in the same way that French women did. Like Jean-Philippe Worth and the great Worth himself, Poiret condemned such slavish copying of the fashion: 'The well dressed woman is the one who picks out her gowns, her adornments, simply because they make her appear more pleasing, not because other people are wearing that style.'[7] Similarly, though he loved strong colours, 'colours of life and poetry', he said that no one should wear such tones if they did not suit her.[8]

As for some of his own creations which with hindsight could be seen to be rather absurd, notably the hobble skirt, Poiret excused himself by saying that there was a spirit of contradiction in fashion which was so frequent and so regular that it could be discovered as a law of the trade. Moreover in the decisions of fashion and of women, there was a sort of provocative challenge to good sense which was really charming, and could only annoy dull minds. Such an appeal could only come from a Frenchman.

He was not a genius in everything he did. As far as the cut and moulding of cloth were concerned, he was outclassed. He made no innovations in construction – many of his dresses were no more than a seam up each side and across the shoulder. The interpretation of a material into a gown that reflects the very nature of that fabric, that fundamental aspect of couture, held no interest for him. He was a man who concentrated on effects, a theatrical director, possessed of imagination and flamboyant display. He was a compound of opposites, sensible in some of his innovations, stupid in others; shrewd in his creation of Martine, reckless and extravagant in his parties and his projects; a patron of young talent, and a conceited advocate of his own genius. He excelled in drama and fantasy, but once the rhapsody had ended he could not come down to earth.

6 The Structure of a Couture House

Before the attempts to make couture houses appear less forbidding and exclusive, which have gathered pace during this century, the accent was on looking as palatial as possible. Most august of all was Maison Worth, which in 1868 was likened to an embassy, staffed with sophisticated young men like attachés with English accents and pearl tie-pins and with a grand apartment, heavy with scent and rich elegance.[1] From this apartment Worth would keep an eye on the rue de la Paix for arriving customers, a custom perpetuated by his son, Jean-Philippe. Any customer of importance was met as soon as she stepped out of the lift by the director himself, with all his *vendeuses* lined up behind him, and would be ushered to a seat to peruse the parading models at her leisure.[2] But behind this salon with its display of svelte efficiency was all the rest of the business, which bustled with activity from the basement to the attics, where the makers of dresses toiled all day and sometimes into the night.

Initially Maison Worth showed many signs of its founder's having begun his career in a textile shop, for many fabrics were placed on display throughout the salons. The first salon showed black and white silks, the second coloured silks, the third velvets and the fourth brocades. All such materials were purchased direct from the manufacturers and saved the customer the chore of going round milliners and mercers herself, which is where Maison Worth was so different from a dressmaker's. The elegant young men on the staff were engaged as salesmen of these materials, under the control of a *premier commis* named Carlsson, who was, like Worth's original partner, a Swede. Princess Metternich thought he did his job splendidly, but the use of four salons to show textiles was not an arrangement which was to be copied by later couture houses. In the event of a customer not liking a material, they preferred to send an underling to fetch other rolls of stuff from the stores rather than having large quantities on show.

Another innovation of Maison Worth which was not followed later was the *salon de lumière*. This was a room lit by gas and with all daylight excluded, so that clients could try on dresses for evening in exactly the same lighting conditions as they would encounter at a ball or dinner party. With the coming of electricity and its use throughout the whole establishment there was no longer the same contrast between day and evening light, so the practice was discontinued, although it had shown an admirable sensitivity in its day. The trend with later houses has been to devote fewer rooms to such activities. They have concentrated on having one or two principal salons where customers can view the collections, keeping the rest of the house for workrooms, rather than having such a princely suite of chambers as Worth had. The rising costs of premises and staff over the years have brought about a retreat from such grandeur.

The humblest member of staff in a couture house was the *arpette*, the apprentice, the girl who picked up the pins. Starting at the age of fourteen or so, she was training to become a seamstress, a member of that company which Poiret called his technicians. She would learn to make stitches like gossamer, to sew seams that were as smooth as liquid and to appreciate that if there were the tiniest mistake the garment in question had to be unstitched and remade, for she was learning the art of perfection. If she made her way over these hurdles, the *arpette* could then become a *deuxième main qualifiée*, a qualified seamstress of the second degree. Above her was the *première main qualifiée*, whom it was her duty to assist in the making of a dress for a client. Both seamstresses were at the service of a fitter, who would direct the *première main* as to what alterations needed doing, after a fitting session with the client. Elsa Schiaparelli, who did not have such a background herself, thought that there could be no better way to understand how to make dresses than to come up this way from apprentice to qualified hand.[3] This was how Madeleine Vionnet began, training as a dressmaker before she ever became a *couturière*, but this was not a route followed by the majority of couturiers, and they are highly dependent on the abilities of their seamstresses. Without their skills no couture house could function.

It has been a feature of the haute couture world that each customer should have her own particular fitter and *vendeuse*, women who would get to know her likes and dislikes and her style, and understand the individual problems of her figure as well as she did herself. Such fitters and *vendeuses* were exclusive to their own group of ladies, and could give them their undivided attention. The *vendeuse* was responsible for the whole order, from the time the customer entered the building and selected a model until that model was made up and delivered, three or more fittings later. With the assistance of a *seconde vendeuse* she had also to ensure that any additional work involved in the dress such as embroidery was completed in time. All such members of the staff had to be modestly dressed, of course, and at the turn of the century and before the First World War the girls wore a uniform consisting of a black skirt and white blouse at both Paquin and Worth.

Another important member of staff, whose duties took her outside the house itself, was the buyer. It was up to her to ensure that the couture house had all the materials it required to operate, such as buttons, trimmings, embroidery and fabrics. She dealt with that considerable sub-structure of small businesses, the makers of decorations and accessories, whose existence made possible Paris's pre-eminence in the world of fashion. Every capital city has its specialist shops, which sell only lace or artificial flowers, but it is the number of such establishments in Paris, each producing its own new lines each season, which gave a designer such enormous choice. Whatever the couturier might require to complete a model, the buyer could go out and find it. Even if he were to demand sea shells or pebbles to decorate a dress, the buyer would find a shop full of such items. So many small enterprises might horrify the economist, for they do not bring down the price of their artifacts by mass production, but in the past the couture houses and their

54 Henri Gervex, 'Paquin at five o'clock', 1906, showing the bustle before closing time. The *vendeuse* kneeling and the *vendeuse* at the table are both showing customers fabrics, while the one on the stairs is bringing in a completed gown. Only four men have dared to enter this temple of femininity.

customers were able to say that the expense was unimportant; only the creation mattered.

Someone who was not concerned with the construction of dresses, but who could well determine whether a gown sold or not, was the house model. Poiret thought that Charles Frederick Worth was the first to use living mannequins in his house instead of wooden dummies, but this was not so. Marie Worth had been a shop model before Worth met her and opened his own establishment, and dressmakers had not been without one or two girls to display frocks in front of customers. What Worth did was to increase the number of girls used. As he made each dress available in several colours and materials, he needed more mannequins to wear them. In addition, the rapid growth in the number of his customers from 1860, the flock of princesses and duchesses that came to his door, made it essential that he have a large number of girls on call to show these ladies his collections. He even went as far as to have a mannequin in his maternity department, as Edmond de Goncourt reported in 1879:

A pretty detail of elegant Parisian life. Amongst the young models, who in the salons of Worth, display and parade upon their svelte bodies the robes of the illustrious couturier, there is a young lady, or rather a woman mannequin, whose speciality is to represent pregnancy in high life.

Seated alone at one side, in the half light of a boudoir, she exhibits to the gaze of those visitors in an interesting condition, the toilette designed with genius for the ungainly enlargement of being with child.[4]

Legend would have it that the very first professional model was Marie Worth, but legend is wrong. Gagelin employed other girls to model at their shop apart from her. What was different about Marie Worth was the way she worked with her husband after their house was opened. Each time that

LE CHOIX DIFFICILE

Manteau du soir de Worth

55 A *vendeuse* describes the qualities of an evening mantle at Maison Worth to a customer and her husband. Both the setting and the presentation are grander than Maison Paquin. 'Le Choix Difficile', April 1914.

Worth sent her to Longchamp or the Bois to display his latest innovation, he was using her as a model outside the privacy of the salon. Hitherto a dressmaker's creations had been exhibited upon the persons of the ladies who bought them and wore them in society; the models only showed dresses at the dressmaker's salon. They were certainly not allowed to wear such finery in the street, but Marie Worth, as wife of a couturier, was one model who could wear the firm's creations wherever she liked. And when she went to Longchamp it was not to see the races or meet her friends, it was to parade her husband's fashions in front of one of the richest gatherings of potential customers in all Paris. She was a walking advertisement, modelling clothes in public with professional skill, and not a customer who might, or might not, show the clothes to advantage. Marie Worth had been trained to wear clothes with as much grace and elegance as possible, and she took such talents out of the salon and into the fashionable world.

During the early 1860s what Mme Worth wore was as important as what the empress or Princess Metternich wore, and sparked off many a new fashion. Jean-Philippe remembered one occasion when his father, tiring of the way in which all the women had gone to a court ball wearing the same very flat head-dresses then in fashion, deliberately went against the fashion and sent Mme Worth with a tall aigrette. Needless to say it immediately started a vogue for such decorations.[5]

In the mid-1860s Marie Worth caught bronchitis and stopped modelling in the salon, but of course whenever she went out, be it to a society wedding or to a ball, she was still showing off her husband's designs. Princess Metternich was of the opinion that Mme Worth was playing at being a great lady, but then it was her job to do precisely that. The daughter of an impoverished tax official, Marie Worth had to mix with the well-born and seem the most elegant and best dressed person present. No salon model ever had to worry about appearing in high society. Perhaps the best description of Marie Worth has been left by the London journalist, F. Adolphus, who met her at Worth's château in 1871. She appeared in a gown of white satin striped with black velvet, a profusion of lace about the shoulders and the discreet gleam of a few diamonds through the lace. Adolphus was overwhelmed; never had he seen a woman so much in harmony with the clothes she was wearing. She and white satin were so completely one that she became the absolute ideal; any other women in white satin could only seem to him to be imposters. As far as Adolphus was concerned she was so sympathetic and so grand that she was like the daughter of a Spanish duke.[6] She gave the role of model a dignity it had not possessed before, and which it has lost since.

There was no recognized system for engaging house models. Paris did not have model agencies before the 1950s, although there were charm schools.[7] Before then any girl who thought she might make a reasonable mannequin had to try her luck by going round all the couture houses until she found a vacancy. Once engaged as promising material she learned the job as she went along. It was not a post for which much intelligence was considered necessary; Poiret had rather a low opinion of his girls. The ideal woman for wearing his clothes was his wife, just as Marie Worth had suited her

56 Marie Worth, the first model to wear haute couture clothes, and to take them outside the privacy of the salon. Photograph taken c.1872/3, seven years after her retirement, by which time she was a grandmother. The well rounded figure was much admired at the period.

husband so well. Nevertheless it was Poiret who took the work of a model a stage further. He did not just send them to Longchamp to show his clothes; he took them on his tours of European capitals, and he had them photographed. Fashion magazines had begun using photographs at the turn of the century, but they engaged young actresses to model the clothes. Following Poiret's example couture models were used more widely in the fashion press, but they never achieved a monopoly, for society ladies, filmstars and the professional photographic models were all used to show clothes in magazines as well. The only time a couture model could expect to make the fashion pages was when the house collections were being photographed.

In the mid-1920s a couture house like Patou employed thirty-two mannequins to model the four hundred and fifty dresses shown at each collection. Jean Patou caused a sensation by sailing to New York and recruiting six American models. The French press immediately declared that this was an insult to French womanhood, but Patou explained that American women were taller than French ones, and it was only right that his

57 Marie Worth's grandson, Jacques Worth, on the right, with a retired seamstress with medal, and eighteen Maison Worth house models, following a fashion show for the American Legion Auxiliary, 15 October 1927.

collections should contain some dresses especially designed for such customers. These American girls were paid 12,000 Poincaré francs a month, and under Patou's advice behaved impeccably, with the result that the attempt by the French press to whip up a scandal came to naught.

The job of the house model was not a glamourous one, and it included periods of both boredom and frenzied activity. She had to be perfectly groomed at all times, ready to show dresses the moment a customer called and then waiting around until the next customer appeared. During the collections she was rushed off her feet, with buyers and private clients wanting to see now this, now that creation. If she worked for the sort of couturier who liked to create clothes upon the body, such as Mme Grès, then she had to stand and pose for hours without complaining. It was hard work and badly paid, but if she were lucky enough to work for a couturier whose establishment rang with enthusiasm, she could have her moments of excitement, wearing the most beautiful clothes in the world.

The head of a fashion house, the god at the top of the whole pyramid, does not come from one particular background. Some we have met already and the rest will follow in later chapters. Couturiers have been as diverse in their paths into fashion as in their characters; no two are fundamentally the same. Some were trained and some were not. Some came from a trading background, others entered the profession without knowing anything about business. Worth, Doucet and Chanel all came from shops; Balmain's aunts had a dress shop, while Balenciaga had his own dressmaking business in Spain before moving to Paris. There have been couturiers who could make fine clothes but who could not draw or design, such as Lucien Lelong and Robert Piguet. On the other hand there have been couturiers who could sketch but who had no idea how to make a dress when they started, such as Dior and Hartnell. Schiaparelli and Lucile both opened with far more hope than experience. More recently couturiers have emerged with more regular training behind them. During the 1940s Hubert de Givenchy was working under such couturiers as Lelong, Piguet, Fath, and Schiaparelli. Balenciaga trained two couturiers who were to blossom in the 1960s, Courrèges and Ungaro. Perhaps the later twentieth century with its fondness for categories will insist on such regular training, but in the past ignorance was not automatically taken as a sign of inability. If the couturier could only draw, then his fitters and cutters worked out the patterns for him. If the couturier could only sew, he could engage designers to produce the ideas. The couture house adapted itself to suit the particular talent of its head. There was no one guaranteed way into the world of couture.

Basically it is the weather which determines how many clothes we shall put on, and it is the rhythm of the seasons which causes us to don or discard particular garments. This natural rhythm was formalized by the upper classes of modern civilization into the social season. It was fashionable to be in town during the spring and early summer but in July one had to go into the country, and the autumn was devoted to hunting and shooting. A lady's wardrobe was dominated by these considerations, which meant that the couture industry had to operate according to the same timetable. It was essential that it should have lots of new designs for the spring, ready for the start of the town season, and it had to have collections of autumn and winter wear ready for the departure of clients into the country. This was not a pattern imposed by the trade, but the response to the seasonal habits of court and aristocracy.

Thus any couturier had to gear himself to a pattern, in the autumn designing clothes for next spring, and in the spring, clothes for next winter. If he or she were wise, he would use the summer lull to accumulate enough ideas to last him through the coming year. Both Charles Frederick and Jean-Philippe Worth found their inspiration in art galleries, while Poiret looked to oriental art. Schiaparelli found her ideas by travelling, as did Alix to some extent. Balenciaga looked to his Spanish roots and ideas from Velazquez.

Callot Soeurs drew on old lace and velvet as their spur to creation. Their sources were as varied as they were themselves, but their designs had all to be ready about the same time.

A couture house was always busy, but the greatest pressures were in the nineteenth and early twentieth centuries when customers required large orders to be carried out very quickly. Every society ball, every dinner party, every first night at the opera, meant a flood of orders descending on the couture houses all at the same time. No one felt the pressures more than Charles Frederick Worth as dominant couturier during the Second Empire and the Third Republic. The court of Napoleon III held three or four state balls per season for four to five thousand guests; the Empress Eugénie gave informal Monday parties for some four hundred guests at a time; the imperial ministers held balls at their ministries, the nobility gave parties at their town houses as did lesser government officials and members of the armed forces, and there was hardly a night during the Paris season without a ball somewhere. In addition there were visits to the theatre, dinners, the opera, and the operetta, for each of which ladies needed new gowns. Thus Maison Worth every season had to supply quantities of evening dresses for its customers, and the announcement of an imperial ball could result in hundreds of orders for evening gowns descending on the house all at once. To cope with such demand the premises were extended with extra floors being added to the top of the building, but for all this there must have been considerable farming-out of orders. It was the custom to buy such items as frills, ruffles, embroidered work, fringes and floral decorations from outside suppliers, so one can see Maison Worth as the centre of a widespread network. The cutting and fitting went on at the rue de la Paix, but the trimmings were brought in ready-made from outside suppliers all over Paris. The fact that Worth still had 1,200 employees in 1871, the year of the lull between the fall of the Second Empire and the establishment of the Third Republic, suggests that he may well have had more before then. Jean-Philippe had 1,200 in 1896, and Mme Paquin 1,000 in the 1900s. Poiret at the height of his success only had one third of this figure, and it was not until after the Second World War that a couture house could really challenge such a number, and the modern couture house with all its branching out into perfumes, cosmetics, furs, boutiques, menswear, textiles and furnishings, is a very different institution from the old couture house which only made clothes.

The conditions suffered by the hundreds of seamstresses involved in this industry did not much concern couture houses in the early days. Worth after all had slept under the counter himself when young, so he did not consider it dreadful that some of his employees might still do so. But the rates of pay were undeniably bad. The clothing industry has a dreadful history of exploitation, particularly in mass production and in the small firms making ready-to-wear. The average Parisian dressmaker's in 1867 might employ between four and forty seamstresses, who were paid on a daily basis, although some were paid by the piece. Their average wage was 2 francs 25 centimes a day, the men in the industry averaging 5 francs a day. This was at a time when an embroidered shawl could cost 300 francs, and a ready-made gown up to 400 francs. Workers in the crinoline industry were slightly better paid at 3 francs 50 centimes to 4 francs a day.[8] The price of a simple couture dress at Worth's was then 1,600 francs, about £64, so it was far out of the reach of the girls who made it.

Such low rates of pay were not a Parisian phenomenon by any means, but a universal feature in the clothing trade. In New York, dressmakers were receiving between 6 and 10 dollars for an eighty-four-hour week in 1900.[9] Such hours were also being worked at a London dressmaker's in 1856. The social reformer, Lord Shaftesbury, had persuaded some dressmakers to reduce their hours voluntarily, but the agreement was not honoured for long. One seamstress was reported as working from 8 a.m. to midnight in her first week at a dressmaker's establishment, but in her second week, when there was a rush of orders from debutantes about to be presented at a royal drawing-room, she worked from 8 a.m. until 3 a.m. next day, and still had to be up at 8 a.m. to work until midnight again. This pattern went on for a month, until the girl was so ill with lack of sleep that she had to leave.[10] Not every girl, however, was in a position to leave, if her family could not support her.

Slowly over the years conditions and pay were improved but not without a fight. There have been several strikes by seamstresses, usually timed to take place on the eve of the collections, which have wrested some improvements from employers. Moreover by the end of the nineteenth century some couturiers were becoming more aware of the need for reform. It was Gaston Worth, first president of the Chambre Syndicale de la Haute Couture Française, who introduced proper insurance and pension schemes at his father's house. His son, Jacques Worth, another president of the Chambre Syndicale, gave the couture industry holidays with pay in 1923. Jacques Worth also oversaw the foundation of the Ecole Supérieure de la Couture, where apprentices for the industry as a whole could be trained from 1930 onwards. This central school was a means of ensuring that the seamstresses produced were of an equal standard throughout the trade.

By 1938 the pay structure at a couture house, in this case Paquin, was as follows. The apprentice started at ten shillings a week, the second hand received 35 shillings a week, and the first hand 45 shillings. The chief male cutter was paid between three and five pounds a week, while the women in the stockrooms got only 35 shillings. The *vendeuse* was on a higher plane since she was paid a salary plus a commission of between $2\frac{1}{2}$ and 5 per cent on each dress sold.[11] The dresses cost upwards of thirty guineas – more than an apprentice earned in a whole year. More recently the Chambre Syndicale has taken on increasing responsibility for supervising improvements throughout the couture industry with welfare, pay, benefits and conditions all coming within its province. The result is that since the Second World War there have been uniform arrangements regarding employees throughout the trade, instead of the old system of each couture house negotiating its own system. There have been many changes in the couture business, both in size and organization, but one thing that has not changed is the structure of the couture house itself, for of course the couturier is still at the top, and the apprentice will always be at the bottom.

58 The most essential worker in haute couture – the seamstress, without whom no design could have been realized. My maternal grandmother who worked for a court dressmaker before her marriage to Lt.Cmdr. Richard Cronin R.N. in 1905. Making her own clothes gave her a reputation for elegance at naval bases, like Chatham.

7 Finance and Promotion

Whilst raising a bank loan might seem the most obvious way in which to finance the foundation of a couture house, this in fact has not been the most common practice. Far more has depended upon assistance from the designer's own family, from friends, acquaintances and contacts. Some houses of course did go to banks. Maison Worth grew out of the bank loans organized on the capital pooled by Worth and his partner Bobergh, the latter investing the larger sum from his savings. Mme Paquin, as mentioned earlier, was married to a banker. Thirdly, there is the example of Pierre Balmain. When he decided to go into business alone at the end of the Second World War, it was Barclay's Bank which found two people willing to invest in him. His third partner, however, was his mother. She sold a bit of land the family had plus such jewellery as she herself possessed, and invested the proceeds in her son, although ten years before she had expressed her doubts about the security of couture as a career for a young man.[1] This sort of support was far more common than that from banks. Couture is a far more risky business than banks usually care for, so the discovery of alternative funds was essential for any aspiring couturier wishing to start his own house.

Norman Hartnell provides another example of family assistance, for when he began, his father paid the rent for the first year at 10 Bruton Street, which gave Hartnell twelve months in which to prove himself. In 1929 Mainbocher started up and his mother was one of the four investors he turned to for funds. When Lucile opened, the little money she had came from her mother, Mrs Kennedy, who also provided the premises in their own house and did some of the sewing and cutting herself, thereby displaying a total commitment to her daughter's enterprise.

A few couturiers actually inherited family couture houses. The Worth dynasty is the most obvious example, with no less than four generations succeeding each other. Creed and Redfern also passed from father to son, while Jacques Doucet inherited his grandmother's shop. Failing a family to assist one, a rich lover can be a great help, as was to occur with Chanel. Where investors were turned to, they were usually found through personal contacts. In addition to financial help from his mother, Mainbocher raised a fund of 40,000 dollars from ladies he already knew from his editorship of *Vogue* – Countess Albert de Munn, Countess Paul de Vallombrosa and Mrs Gilbert White, as well as contributing his own savings. When Hardy Amies began his business, it was his friend, Lady Jersey, who introduced him to a friend of hers with money to invest.

There have been couturiers who slowly saved up their earnings in other spheres or whilst working lower down the couture scale. Balenciaga built up his sum of £10,000 by saving as much as he could from his little dress business in Spain. Mme Vionnet slowly acquired savings of 100,000 francs from working for other people for nearly twenty years, but she still had to have two investors to provide an additional 200,000 francs before she could open her business. Others started in a small way to begin with. Jeanne Lanvin's house grew out of the slowly increasing demand for her children's clothes, an activity which had been confined originally to her family circle. Jean Patou began with a small dress shop of his own and converted himself into a couturier proper after war service as a captain gave him a bit more capital. Schiaparelli started making clothes in the attic where she lived. Poiret opened a shop in the first instance, and built himself up from that. Jacques Fath started with just one fitter and himself in 1937.

A small beginning was the common foundation, regardless of where the money was found. The sums invested were often modest, and the couturier could only expand his house after he had started selling clothes in some quantities. The great exception to all the other couture houses was Maison Dior. Christian Dior was working as a designer in the house of Lelong in 1945, when an acquaintance from his home town in Normandy asked if he knew of a designer who might go to the assistance of a small couture business called Clarence. It was owned by the textile magnate, Marcel Boussac, who was in cotton, and he wished to revive its fortunes. Dior was reluctant to go to another employer and said that he would only leave his own job as designer if it was to begin his own couture house. As Dior already possessed several years' experience working in couture, Boussac decided he would agree to Dior's proposals and give him the money to open on his own. The house of Dior was granted an investment of 10 million old francs in 1946, from the wealth of the Boussac industrial empire. As Dior's first collections were such a success, this sum was increased to 100 million old francs by 1949.[2] This was a scale of investment unparalleled in couture history; no other couturier had the power of a whole industry behind him from the very start.

In 1948 Hardy Amies went to see this new French house, which was already overspilling its original premises, and was amazed at the power which stood behind it. No English couture house could ever hope for such enormous backing from industry. It was not simply the money, either, for Boussac also provided Dior with its economic experts to manage the business, and the vast financial expertise of the industrial firm was at the disposal of the couture house whenever it was needed. It was all this industrial expertise which set up Dior Perfumes and Dior Furs in 1947 and started the licensing system for the use of the Dior name on ties, hosiery, gloves, hats, knitwear, lingerie and girdles. Other couturiers initiated expansion into boutiques and licensed associations only after some years in the business, but Maison Dior had such extensions only one year after opening. Behind Dior there was an industrial giant which knew how to make money and how to capitalize on a designer with talent. After the Second World War international industry began to move into the ownership of couture houses on an increasing scale.

This is not to say that some textile firms did not give some support before. Hardy Amies had some backing from the Linton Tweed Mills in

Cumberland, but it was not on the scale of the Boussac empire. Charles Frederick Worth did so much to promote the Lyon textile industry that it would be very surprising if the Chambre de Commerce had not shown its gratitude by helping to build up his business, although the house records do not survive to show how much money may have been involved.

Some couturiers did very well, of course, without huge financial backing. Mainbocher's annual turnover in 1929–30 was 16 million francs, and by 1939 he had increased it to 100 million francs. Chanel was doing so well by 1930 that she was reputed to be paying $17\frac{1}{2}$ million francs in taxes.[3] Her turnover that year was 120 million francs, and rumour had it that she had some £3 million banked in London. Of course she did have the exceedingly rich Duke of Westminster as an ardent admirer, who could provide financial know-how from his own team of experts on how best to manage one's money. Jacques Fath had been to business school before he turned to couture, so he was his own financial expert. Not only did he establish such related branches as hats, perfumes, and a boutique, but he initiated unprecedented relations with the manufacturers of ready-to-wear clothing. He began this by designing a collection for the American ready-to-wear industry in 1948, and just before his early death in 1954 he had made an agreement with the French textile producer Jean Prouvost to start a 'Fath Université' range of ready-to-wear for the French market, based on the American pattern.[4] This was the sort of business about which the rest of the haute couture world was very haughty. Clothes for the masses were not a matter with which it had ever sullied its fingers. Poiret had been the only one to propose relations with the cheaper market, and that had only been when he was desperate for business. Nevertheless Fath was a prophet in foreseeing the expansion of mass clothing in the 1950s and in realizing that here was a market which was going to overwhelm the couture industry in the scale of its financial activity. More recently, of course, the couture houses have changed their attitudes completely and have been falling over themselves in order to become involved with the wealthy *prêt-à-porter* roundabout.

Selling clothes has long been an important part of the French economic system. The production of clothing for women throughout France was estimated to be worth £4 million (100 million francs) in 1864, of which 40 per cent was made in Paris. Only one sixth of this amount was for export, and the sort of garments that were principally exported were several types of wraps such as *paletots*, *talmas*, *pelisses* and *mantelets*, and embroidered shawls, dresses, hoods and children's clothing. At that date there was also a thriving industry making crinoline cages and crinoline petticoats to an annual value of £800,000 of which half was exported.[5] As the century progressed the value of French clothing exports increased. In 1898 clothing for both sexes and lingerie was exported for 91.8 million francs and rose by 1899 to 142.5 million francs. In 1912 the value of exported confections for women alone was worth 157.181 million francs and by 1913 had increased to 158.074 million francs.[6] In 1914 Jean-Philippe Worth could state that Paris earned 50 million dollars a year for couture dresses and modes.

The First World War caused a setback in this pattern of rising sales to foreigners, but in the 1920s the couture trade flourished and soon made up the loss. It was employing 250,000 employees in 2,000 workrooms, salons and shops by 1927, and the value of haute couture exports was 5,750,000 francs, equal to one tenth of total French world trade.[7] From this peak it plummeted when the effects of the Wall Street crash in 1929 hit Paris. Foreign buyers cancelled orders, private customers declined in number and stores reduced their requirements. Ten thousand couture employees were thrown out of work. There was a slow recovery by the late 1930s but then came the Second World War, and a boom in couture exports did not come again until 1947.

Trade is greatly helped by advertising, but haute couture only became involved in such promotion of its product very slowly. Whilst Worth's very first designs were advertised by his employers, Gagelin, when he opened his own house he only advertised in the trade press. The great deterrent to publishing illustrations of new dresses was the rampant piracy of the day. Dressmakers copied the engravings in fashion magazines, so if a couture house allowed a dress to be illustrated it might be reproduced hundreds of times over without the couturier receiving a penny for it. The theft of designs was also current. In 1869 a set of one dozen fashion plates was published by G. Jannes as *La Mode Artistique*, one of which is identical with an original sketch in the Worth archives. These plates were then copied in the United States by *Harper's Bazar* (sic) in May and July of that year, without acknowledgments to Jannes or to Worth. In addition there was the use of a couturier's name without his permission. A Maison Worth in London in the 1880s had nothing to do with the Paris house, and Poiret, as seen earlier, found his name being used in New York. Thus a couture house faced many difficulties in the promotion field, and had to weigh the advantage of publicizing its products against the loss that would ensure in the unlicensed reproductions of its designs. If a woman could get a Paris dress copied by her local dressmaker, she was not going to send an order to Paris for the original creation.

Examples of Worth gowns did occur in the fashion press in the 1870s, but it was not until the 1880s that the house took the decision to promote its wares itself. As so much of its custom now came from abroad, it was necessary to arouse foreigners' interest and keep the name of the house before their eyes. It is noticeable that the magazines chosen by Maison Worth were not the usual fashion papers, but more esteemed journals such as *L'Art et la Mode* and the semi-political *L'Illustration*. In England it was the serious journal, *The Woman's World*, edited by Oscar Wilde, which carried the officially approved Worth illustrations (see fig 17). This demonstrates the august standing of Maison Worth at that time. It was not until 1891 that Worth allowed the regular illustration of its clothes in a fashion magazine proper, and this was *Harper's Bazar*. The accent on excellence was maintained by engaging the best fashion artist of the day, Sandoz, and such engravers as Méaulle and Jonnard, to ensure that the illustrations were the very best in the fashion press. In addition, the hairstyles of the models were always by Lenthéric, to keep the emphasis on quality.

Photographs of couture clothes became regular features of such maga-

zines as *Les Modes* at the very start of this century. They brought the same headaches as ordinary engravings in that they could be copied just as easily, so before releasing photographs of new clothes to the fashion press, the couture trade was to insist that publication did not occur until after the collections had been seen by customers and buyers. Any magazine which broke this instruction would be denied couture photographs thereafter.

An innovation in the sphere of advertising came in 1912 when the publisher, Lucien Vogel, persuaded several couture houses to provide financial backing for a new fashion magazine, to be sold in a limited edition. He had been very impressed by some watercolours done by Bernard Boutet de Monvel and Pierre Brissaud, both graduates of the Ecole des Beaux Arts, where Vogel had studied architecture. Poiret's two publications had set a precedent in showing just how charming a magazine could be when fully illustrated by artists, avoiding photography altogether. Vogel now engaged Poiret's two illustrators, Paul Iribe and Georges Lepape, for his new magazine, and also recruited Georges Barbier, Jean Besnard, A.E. Marty, and Charles Martin, as well as de Monvel and Brissaud.

The finance for the magazine was provided by the leading houses, Worth, Chéruit, Doeuillet, Doucet, Lanvin, Poiret and Redfern. At first there was some resistance from the illustrators. Being all original artists, they felt they were above the mere copying of clothes, but Vogel persuaded them to co-operate by giving them complete control of the design of the magazine as a whole, plus a share of the profits. They were allowed to introduce whatever decorative features they liked providing they also illustrated the dresses, and to keep the latter interesting they could show them in situations with captions. The outcome was one of the most delightful publications in fashion history, with coloured plates of dresses interspersed with articles adorned with decorative arrangements of accessories, presenting an image of the total look of the mode. The *Gazette du Bon Ton*, as it was known, ceased publication in 1914 on the outbreak of war, issued one copy in 1915, and resumed regular publication in 1920. In 1921 it was bought up by Condé Nast, owner of *Vogue* in the United States, who continued to publish it until 1925. The *Gazette du Bon Ton* was unique in being financed originally by the couture houses themselves, for they did not repeat the exercise.[8] More recently the charms of the *Gazette du Bon Ton* have been its undoing. With its plates in demand by print-sellers, copies of the magazine have been torn up for their plates, and all the rest of the copy with its delightful illustrations around articles has been consigned to the dustbin – hardly the way to treat a magazine which was a work of art throughout.

The dominant fashion magazines in those years were privately owned. *Harper's Bazar* began in New York in November 1867 and was owned by the publishers, Harper and Brothers. It founded its British number *Harper's Bazaar* in 1929. American *Vogue* started in 1893, and began its British edition in 1916, and its French one in 1922. In addition to paying for advertisements in these fashion papers, couture houses would receive free publicity whenever a fashion magazine decided to do a feature on them, and this could lead to disputes when a house felt that it was not getting enough editorial coverage. When *Vogue* became the dominant fashion journal after

59 The entry of officially approved couture advertisements in the fashion press; a Worth evening gown of sky blue satin, edged with black fur and embroidered with beads; hair by Lenthéric, 1894.

APRÈS L'ONDÉE

Robe de dîner de Worth

60 Haute couture's own magazine, *Gazette du Bon Ton*, used drawings in preference to photographs. Worth's dinner gown 'Après L'Ondée', illustrated by A. Lorenzi, April 1913.

the First World War, it was to encounter this sort of complaint. In 1923, for instance, Jacques Worth was annoyed because he felt *Vogue* was not giving enough editorial mention to his house although he paid for advertisements in it. He was also worried that his house was too closely associated with the old guard, and wanted to attract much younger custom and money. The editor responded by asking Worth to dress her daughter, who came out that year.

Vogue also suffered from rivalry between couturiers, most notably Patou's jealous resentment of Chanel's success. He would assiduously count the amount of space which the magazine gave to Chanel, and if it was more than he was receiving, would bombard the editor with complaints about such 'injustice'. In the end *Vogue* had to inform Patou that it gave him better coverage than any other magazine, without his ever having expressed one word of thanks, and eventually he apologized. Patou had over-reacted, but a couturier did have to watch his magazine coverage for it gave him free publicity, and when an editor reduced mention of a house or dropped its name completely, it was a serious matter, a danger signal that the house had ceased to be newsworthy and was slipping out of the big league.

Although haute couture fashions were intended for the wealthy, *Vogue* in the 1930s did attempt to broaden their appeal by introducing features on budget dressing. British *Vogue* in October 1937 indicated that working girls on £5 a week might dress very smartly in English ready-to-wear versions of Parisian fashion for £50 a year. This figure was what a woman about-town might spend on her clothes for a season, and a girl going on a cruise might buy her casual wear and evening dresses for the same sum. The benefit to haute couture of an increase in public interest came through the manufacturers of ready-to-wear expanding their orders for couture *toiles* and patterns.

Another method of encouraging the general public's interest in high fashion was for couturiers to participate in international exhibitions. The nineteenth century saw an enormous number of such trade fairs. Apart from the 1851 and 1862 exhibitions in London, there were similar large-scale presentations in Paris in 1855, 1867, 1878, 1888 and 1900, others in Vienna and Berlin, and the American centenary exhibition at Philadelphia in 1876. These shows had sections devoted to such natural products as wool, silk and cotton, and to the artifacts made from them. Thus the Paris Exposition Universelle of 1867 had displays of lace, fans, gloves, corsets, crinolines, lingerie, embroidery, bonnets, shirts, shoes and clothing. The *grand prix* was awarded to the city of Lyon for all the institutions it had created to advance the silk industry, while the Chambre de Commerce received a gold medal for its quality silks. The firm of Doucet, still in its pre-couture days, was awarded a bronze medal for its babyclothes. It might be thought that couturiers would have been interested in exhibiting their creations at these mammoth fairs from the very start, but in fact their approach was gradual and cautious. Worth, as seen in chapter 1, won prizes in 1851 and 1855 when at Gagelin, but once he was his own master he did not participate in such exhibitions. What worried couturiers, of course, was the old problem of piracy. As with publishing, a dress shown to the public could be copied. There were professional spies, employed by dressmakers, who were sent out with sketchbooks and later with cameras to record a new fashion as soon as it stepped out of a couture house. These spies were mainly women, who frequented such smart rendezvous as restaurants, the races, garden parties and balls in order to see what society ladies were wearing, and then rushed back to their employers with sketches of the best clothes to reproduce. Putting the latest couture models in a public exhibition therefore would only have widened the opportunity for fashion spies.

When the couturiers did decide to risk the showing of clothes at exhibitions, what they put on display were good clothes rather than trend-

THE DRESSMAKERS' SPIES: STEALING THE FASHIONS.

Drawn by René Lelong.

HUNTING THE NEW MODELS: THE UNDERHAND NOTING OF THE LATEST FASHIONS IN PARIS.

61 A couturier must keep his latest models secret, but as soon as they are worn in public the spies employed by lesser dressmakers copy them with notebooks and cameras. 'The Dressmakers' Spies: stealing the fashions', drawing by René Lelong, July 1909.

setting fashions. The occasion was the Exposition Universelle in Paris in 1900. With couture being an important part of French exports, the government wanted some sort of participation by the couturiers, and they responded by presenting the first joint exhibition of haute couture. The houses which took part were Worth, Callot Soeurs, Doeuillet, Paquin and Redfern, together with some lesser establishments. The display was in spacious salons lit by electric light, with the clothes mounted on wax figures.

This was the first time that the general public in France had the opportunity to study couture clothes at its leisure. In normal circumstances such garments might be glimpsed in the street as the wearer drove past in a carriage or passed from her coach into a great house for a ball, but now at the exhibition the visitors could stand and stare. What drew the greatest crowds was Worth's presentation of a lady preparing to attend an English court reception, for it contained the most magnificent examples of that house's work, resplendent evening gowns heavy with embroidery and appliqué work and sweeping court trains in scarlet velvet. In addition to this, Worth showed a fur coat and townswear, while other houses presented dinner gowns, ball gowns, town dresses, reception gowns and court wear. Henceforth participation in international fairs became regular practice. In 1910 in Brussels and in 1915 in San Francisco, couture clothes were being shown to a wider public than ever before. There was perhaps a whiff of democratization in letting the people see the best clothes in the world, for a

Robe de diner
Callot Sœurs

Robe de bal dentelle blanch
Modèle de G. Dœuillet & Cⁱᵉ

few years before the couture houses would not have dreamt of showing their treasures to the plebs.

After the First World War the presentation of couture was more closely related to other movements in contemporary art. Poiret's view that dress was part of the applied arts was fully expressed at the Art Deco exhibition in Paris in 1925. The new, simple, streamlined clothes conveyed the spirit of the machine age, and were as clean cut as tubular steel. In 1937 haute couture took part in the Exposition Internationale des Arts et Techniques in Paris, with their clothes displayed in the 'pavilion of elegance'. The Chambre Syndicale de la Haute Couture arranged for garments to be displayed on elongated plaster figures so typical of 1930s' taste. One couturier rebelled against it – Schiaparelli. She detested the plaster figure provided, and rather than show her clothes on that, buried it in turf and arranged her creations along a clothes line. This joky gesture, so characteristic of her, entertained the crowds considerably.

62 *Left* The first public exhibition of haute couture models in a static presentation open to all, organized by the Collectivité de la Couture, Exposition Universelle, Paris 1900. Dinner gown by Callot Sœurs with appliquéd lace.

63 *Right* Dœuillet's exhibit, a ball gown of white lace upon a pink ground.

Robe de ville taffetas framboise
Modèle de Paquin

Robe de réception drap broc[...]
Modèle de Redfern

64 *Left* Paquin's exhibit, a town dress in raspberry taffeta.

65 *Right* A Redfern entry, reception gown of grey Liberty satin embroidered with silvery grey wool.

Paris couture declined to participate in the World's Fair at New York in 1939, giving as its reason that clothes put on long display would be out of date within a month of arrival. Perhaps another reason was that New York already had budding designers of its own, and Paris did not want such rivals to get a good look at the secrets of its creations.

The Second World War put a stop to such international festivals for the next few years, but immediately the war was over the Chambre Syndicale de la Haute Couture set about organizing a travelling exhibition, the Théâtre de la Mode, which was sent to the United States to show that Paris couture was still alive and kicking. The clothes were mounted on wire models in a lively manner, with examples from all the leading houses. This exhibition in particular shows couture using public display as a means of promoting its trade. This was the fundamental reason for participating in such presentations, weighing the advantage of increased publicity and sales against the danger of unlicensed copying.

Robe satin blanc voilé
Modèle de Worth

66 An entry from Jean-Philippe Worth, an evening gown that is the ultimate in luxury. White satin veiled with pink muslin, covered with black tulle, appliquéd with cloud shapes of black velvet and crêpe, and striped from neck to hem with diamonds, in a pattern of clouds and rain.

8 The Clientele and Their Clothes

The reason why ladies in high society needed a large wardrobe of expensive clothes was not simply a matter of personal choice. It was expected of them both by the court and by their contemporaries. When Professor N.W. Senior, a specialist in political economy, was visiting Paris in 1857 gathering material for a book, he made some inquiries regarding the cost of clothes and what was demanded of a lady by the Empress Eugénie and by life in Parisian society. His hostess, Mme Circout, answered: 'The Empress is said to have a wonderful memory, and to display it by reminding people that she has already expressed her admiration of a particular dress, which is supposed to be a hint that she ought not to see it again. They say she seldom wears a gown twice.'[1] Thus any woman attending court who did not wish to incur an imperial rebuke, however politely put, did not wear the same dress on more than one occasion.

The position was exactly the same in England, for the Prince of Wales once growled at Georgina, third Marchioness of Salisbury, that he had seen her dress before, although that very brave lady retorted that he would also be seeing it again.[2] This requirement by courts meant that ladies had to wear new clothes for every occasion to which they were invited. The problem was even worse if they were invited to stay at court for a few days. When the French imperial court was at Fontainebleau in the summer, persons in favour would be invited to spend a week there, which of course involved them in considerable expense. Prosper Merimée told Professor Senior of a friend, by no means rich, who was invited to Fontainebleau for seven days, so she had to have fifteen new gowns, two for each day plus one for accidents. Autumn the court spent at Compiègne, when one hundred guests would be invited for eight days. Princess Metternich used to take eighteen dresses to these gatherings, although some ladies took as many as twenty-four. In England *Punch* advised ladies going to spend a week in the country at a stately home to take at least three dresses for each day. No wonder Worth became so rich.

In addition to the requirements of the court there were those of life in high society. Anyone participating in the Season had to have a suitable wardrobe for all the events involved. As the nineteenth century progressed the number of garments required increased. In Paris in the 1860s a lady needed dresses and jackets for the morning, afternoon gowns for visiting and taking tea, and then evening gowns for dinners, balls, the theatre and opera. When staying in the country of course, a riding habit had to be included. By the 1880s four gowns a day were necessary. When Lady Ottoline Morrell was a girl at Welbeck Abbey, the seat of her half-brother, the sixth Duke of Portland, aristocratic dowagers with marriageable daughters would descend

67 One essential item for country weekends, English tailor-made suits for shooting or walking, 1908.

for visits. These *grandes dames* would come down to breakfast in velvet gowns with laced fronts, change into tweed suits to drive to lunch with the men out shooting, come back and change into satin teagowns from Paris for tea time, then change once more into the elaborate brocades and velvets of full evening dress for dinner.[3] More sporting ladies who did hunt or shoot would have had to change into appropriate clothes in the morning, a riding habit or the ankle or calf-length shooting skirt, instead of the tweed suits. The increasing sporting activities for women added further specialized garments to the wardrobe – for golf, tennis and yachting. Thus a woman in society might be confronted with the need to change her clothes as many as five or six times a day.

As at court most of these clothes had to be new. It might be possible to get away with a tweed suit that was a year old when tramping round muddy fields, but not indoors, when each lady had to look as splendid as possible (within the bounds of good taste). As noted in chapter 2, women were expected to reflect their husbands' wealth and position, so all this dressing up, the new clothes and jewels were all a marital duty, a silent advertisement of status.

The disposal of these clothes followed a long-established tradition. It was customary for courts to pass on clothing to ladies-in-waiting and to servants; indeed, these recipients regarded such gifts as their particular right, and there could be trouble if any servants felt that they were not getting their established due. With the Empress Eugénie never wearing a dress twice in public, the disposal of her garments became a small industry. Some were given away in return for favours done, but most passed through the hands of her ladies-in-waiting, who sold them. Theatres were one sphere where 'old' royal garments were welcome; they had been buying imperial cast-offs for generations, as it was an easy way of obtaining splendid additions for their wardrobes. A particularly nineteenth-century development was the sale of imperial gowns to dress-hire agencies. Such agencies were not new but the number greatly increased, especially in the United States with the rise both in population and in the proportion of people finding their way into the upper reaches of the middle class. Thus a gown worn by the Empress Eugénie at a ball in Paris might end up a few months later on a Southern belle in Louisiana.

Naturally servants also sold the clothes they were given, as they were usually too luxurious for their own use. There were scores of shops in those days dealing in second- or third-hand clothing, for not only were new clothes too expensive for much of the population, but the range of ready-made garments was very limited, so that for many the best chance of finding something suitable without having to have it made up, was to look among the second-hand goods. The number of such shops did not diminish with the advent of the twentieth century; in 1914 Jean-Philippe Worth complained that there had been an increase. It was not until after the First World War, when far more women were wage-earning, that the demand for well made, new, ready-to-wear clothing really got under way.[4]

Between the wars the fashionable lady still had to have a considerable wardrobe and change several times a day. Once having breakfasted in her

68 The disposal of clothes. Detail of a machine-made lace evening skirt created for Empress Eugénie by Worth in 1864 and later given by her to her distant relative Mme Thomas de Leval.

negligée she would don either a morning frock and coat or a tailored suit. These were usually of tweed or wool in winter and linen in summer, and were worn when a lady was attending to business or calling at shops to leave her orders for them to deliver to her house later. After lunch she would have to change into something more elaborate for afternoon calls, an afternoon frock of velvet or fine wool if it were cool, or of chiffon or crêpe in summer. In the 1930s evening meant a further change into long skirts. If going to cocktails or dinner, she wore a dinner gown or suit of velvet or satin, sometimes with a fanciful little hat. If going to the theatre or a nightclub she wore an evening dress of crêpe, silk, satin or chiffon. When out of town she added sporting clothes, while a new feature of the twenties and thirties was the vogue for sunbathing, which entailed having beach clothes for smart resorts and not just bathing costumes. To supply this new demand Worth opened boutiques at Biarritz and at Cannes, as well as at 221 Regent Street. The period also saw winter sports becoming fashionable, so an additional wardrobe was necessary for ski resorts. The thirties introduced the picture frock, a long gown in crêpe, chiffon or organdie for wearing at garden parties and at the most important race meetings at Longchamp and Royal Ascot, but not at Goodwood. In addition to all these clothes there were travelling outfits throughout the whole period of this study, for not only did the rich travel from town to country and back, but there were also weekends at the homes of celebrated hosts. The richest Englishman of all, the Duke of Westminster, was always on the move, rarely staying more than three weeks in one place, with all his private cars, his train and yachts conveying the lady guests with their mountains of luggage.

The size of these wardrobes meant a considerable sub-structure of staff to deal with them. Quite apart from ladies' maids to dress their mistresses, there had to be relays of servants to transport the cases. When the French imperial train conveyed the guests to Compiègne, each lady having an average of twenty dress cases, the luggage ran into several hundred items. It was a veritable mountain which piled up in the palace courtyard until servants and chamberlains got the guests and their luggage sorted out. Nowadays such a scale of transportation is confined mostly to heads of state.

In order to pay for these quantities of clothes a lady had to have a dress allowance. The amount would depend upon her husband's or father's wealth, and there was considerable variation between what the very grand could command and what those on the fringes of high society could afford. This was a question which interested Professor Senior in 1857, and he asked what it would cost the wife of a professional man to dress in Paris. The answer was 10,000 francs (£400) for Mrs Senior, and about 3,000 or 4,000 francs for their daughter (£120 to £160). It was cheaper for the unmarried woman for she did not pay morning visits or dine out in the evening. The professor also attended a reception at the British Embassy and asked Lady Cowley, the ambassadress, about the cost of the ladies' evening gowns. She replied that the expense lay in the region of 1,000 to 1,200 francs (£40 to £48).[5] As will be remembered, clothes at Worth were to cost even more, with the simplest day dress priced at £60 in the 1860s. Such prices Professor Senior considered would be ruinous for a man of moderate fortune.

MILLIONNAIRESSES.

Mrs. A. "WELL, GOOD-BYE, DEAR. YOU MUST COME AND SEE MY NEW DRESSES FROM PARIS—ONE *CHARMING* MORNING DRESS, AMONG OTHERS, QUITE SIMPLE, AND ONLY COST SIXTY-SEVEN GUINEAS! YOU'LL COME, WON'T YOU? AND TELL ME WHAT YOU THINK OF IT!"

Mrs. B. "O, MY DEAR, I'M NO JUDGE OF CHEAP CLOTHING, YOU KNOW!"

The significance of these prices can be seen by comparing them with incomes in the mid-nineteenth century. An Englishman was considered wealthy if he had £5,000 a year. The professional man or merchant might earn around £500 a year, and a worker around £50 a year. Agricultural labourers were among the worst off, with a farmworker and his wife and children earning all together about £48 a year in the Midlands but only £28

69 The cost of clothes, August 1873.

a year in Devon.[6] Thus the price of a Paris dress was often more than the ordinary working man earned in a whole year, and was still too expensive for the professional classes as well. The gentleman with £6,000 a year would have an estate and some seventeen servants, and he might manage a dress allowance of £400 a year for his wife, but the numbers of such persons were comparatively few. Under the schedule D taxation system there were only 42,000 people in England and Wales with incomes of £1,000 to £5,000 a year, and 7,500 people with incomes in excess of £5,000.[7] Even these were small fry compared with the magnates and royalty who went to Worth's, for their incomes could run into five and six figures.

In 1871 Charles Frederick Worth could state that while a Parisian lady spending £60 a year on her clothes did not look too bad, his customers spent anything from £400 to £4,000 a year on his creations. The people who paid such sums were mainly Russian nobility, and American millionaires, with the occasional Peruvian or Chilean magnate. In the main his English and French ladies were less extravagant, and he could not recall a single example of a German customer spending as much as £4,000 in the space of one year. Such figures represent the summit of nineteenth-century society. Maison Worth's customers were simply the richest people in the world. And it should be born in mind that these sums only represent the dress allowance, for a lady would also have accounts for shoes, accessories and so forth. The rich woman could easily spend £150 a year on shoes alone, so her expenditure on her whole appearance could total anything from £500 to £5,000 a year – in other words the complete income of even a moderately wealthy man. No wonder Professor Senior considered such figures ruinous.

How a woman of moderate wealth was to manage can be seen in a study of 1902. Given that her allowance was worth £200 a year and her personal maid could also run up garments when needed, she was advised to budget as follows: £40 for lingerie, including four new dressing gowns a year, plus silk petticoats and two corsets. A good tweed suit costing nine or ten guineas was an investment that should last two or three years. She would make a considerable saving by making her own muslin dresses for £5, and should only buy four new dresses a year: a smart gown in, say, black for 16 guineas, for which the maid should make a blouse so that the skirt could be worn separately without the bodice, a winter gown of wool for £6 and two evening dresses in satin or silk at around 16 guineas and £12. For outdoors an evening wrap at £15 was necessary, and a country wrap at £5. She should allow £15 for blouses and shirts and £10 for boots and shoes. A mackintosh would cost £3 and an umbrella three guineas. Hats should not exceed £15. If the lady wished to ride, that was an additional expense which could not be managed on £200, so an extra £60–£70 would be needed.[8]

These prices could be contrasted with some of those being charged by the English couture house, Lucile. Her nightdresses were 10–12 guineas each, and her fur coats up to £3,000. When she opened her New York branch in 1910 she was charging 400 dollars (£80) for evening gowns and 4,000 dollars (£800) for evening wraps. An afternoon gown sold at 300 dollars (£60) and an afternoon wrap at 400 dollars, while a parasol cost 100 dollars (£20). This was the time when conspicuous consumption by the rich had reached its

MATRIMONIAL SPECULATIONS.

He: I'm afraid I couldn't make you happy, darling, on $2,000 a year.
She: Oh, it's plenty! With economy I can dress on $1,500; and just think, dear, we can have all the rest for household expenses!

apogee, with money being lavished on marble mansions, foreign villas, yachts, Rolls Royces, gargantuan banquets, grandiose balls, extravagant fancy dress parties, opulent house parties, tours, shoots, races and hunting, quite apart from jewels and couture clothes. In bleak contrast the middle class, from its lower to its upper levels, was earning between £160 and £700 a year, while the average working man, if he were lucky enough to have a job, was earning up to £77 a year, and the working woman received a mere £35 for the same hours. Thus a working class woman would have had to labour for eighty-five years to earn the price of a Lucile fur coat, assuming she could live that long. Even if she did manage to acquire such a coat, it would not fit, for the poor were on average five inches shorter than the rich, owing to bad housing, inadequate diets and the long hours of work they endured.[9]

The Great War brought one benefit for women in that they were paid higher wages for doing men's jobs. Girls on munition work, the most dangerous, could earn as much as £5 a week, and as a result they were better fed and better dressed than women of their status had ever been. Nevertheless the gap between their earnings and the cost of couture clothes

70 The need for a dress allowance. In English terms he earned £400 a year, and she was asking for a dress allowance of £300 a year, 1898.

remained enormous. During the twenties and thirties, however, the situation changed considerably. Thanks to Poiret, clothes were becoming simpler. The elaborate Edwardian evening gown of satin, covered with net, overlaid with tulle and bedecked with embroidery and appliqué work, was being replaced by gowns of much simpler construction using only one piece of material. Because of this, couture clothes between the wars were not so fearfully expensive as they had been before and could cost half the price of a Worth gown back in the 1860s.

At the English house of Reville in the 1920s an afternoon dress of navy-blue taffeta cost £16, while a gown of gold and blue tissue, which was much favoured at that time but which was very impractical as it creased so easily, cost £18. In a smaller couture house like Lachasse prices would be lower. In 1934 Lachasse charged ten and a half guineas for a suit, which was increased to 16 guineas by 1937, while one of its evening gowns could be had for 18 guineas. At the same date a very simple suit from Molyneux was priced at 22 guineas. A Schiaparelli blouse costing eight guineas was considered extremely expensive in 1937. To order a couture gown from Paquin in 1938 cost from 30 to 40 guineas for evening wear, compared with three or four guineas for a ready-made gown in a good department store. At the coronation of George VI the Duchess of Westminster wore a London-made gown of ivory-coloured lace embroidered all over with mother of pearl sequins. It cost £40 and even she considered that outrageously expensive. After the Second World War prices doubled. A day dress in 1947 cost £80, and embroidered or fur-trimmed garments from £250.

A dress allowance of £500 a year was about the limit for a lady in the 1930s, and allowed her to purchase many couture creations. The average male teacher in 1938, in contrast, was earning £331 a year. When Lady Mountbatten was a teenager she had an allowance of £300 a year from her grandfather, but that was exceptional. An allowance of about £40 or £50 was more usual for girls in high society before they came out, and this had to cover all clothing, travel, tips and sundries. They tended to be dressed on the cheap, with fabrics bought at the sales and run up by the local little dressmaker. It was when they came out that the bills started soaring.

Not every lady chose to be dressed by the greatest names in Paris. Some favoured lesser known couturiers who made good clothes without featuring in the fashion magazines. Thus Princess Alice, Countess of Athlone, who had a reputation for elegance, patronized Mme Roland in Paris. When her husband was appointed Governor General of Canada in 1940, all the princess's wardrobe came from Mme Roland, the last consignment she received from her before the war. In 1946 Princess Alice transferred her custom to Worth of London for her best wear, but she had an excellent French maid, trained by Mme Roland, who made her ordinary wear. The possession of a good maidservant was essential to the well-dressed woman. As seen in 1902 a personal maid who could run up a dress was an invaluable asset, for the clothes were far from practical, requiring repairs, adjustments and sometimes replacements. Most evening wear in the 1920s and 1930s was of pure silk, which looked very beautiful but which got very creased. An experienced lady's maid who could iron them out every time they were worn

"INTENSIVE" PLEASURES OF THE SEASON : A DÉBUTANTE'S RECREATIONS.

SPECIALLY DRAWN FOR "THE ILLUSTRATED LONDON NEWS" BY STEVEN SPURRIER, R.O.I.

FROM DIVING TO MANNEQUIN PARADE AND POLO MATCH : A PICTURED DIARY OF SOCIAL PLEASURES.

71 A debutante's clothing needs in 1925, a swimsuit at the Bath Club, a tennis frock for Ranelagh, a frock for a day by the river, a frock for watching polo at Hurlingham, and most essential of all regular visits to a couture house to select the right wardrobe. Drawing by Steven Spurrier, June 1925.

was to be treasured.

If the world of haute couture was exclusive as far as its prices were concerned, it was not so as regards class and social rank. When Worth first soared to success, jealous critics tried to make out that only the noblest-born could pass through his portals and that would-be customers needed letters of credence as if they were ambassadors, but this was pure invention. As Charles Dickens wrote, 'the man-milliner professes to know no distinction nor degree. He is open to all, like the law.' A plain Mrs could see Worth as much as any princess, providing she made an appointment – and providing she had the money. In fact contemporaries were amazed at the wide range of

women who went to Worth's, for not only did it include all the empresses in Europe, the aristocracy and the diplomatic corps, but any *nouveau riche* industrialist's wife was welcome, and so were successful actresses and the most sensational courtesans.

The empresses came to Worth for fashionable wear, for court dress and for coronation clothes. What they wore had to be comparatively conservative and respectable, as well as grand. Undoubtedly the Russian court was the most extravagant and lavish, although not every consort on the czarist throne was as immoderate in her dressing as were some of the grand duchesses and princesses. The Empress Maria Alexandrovna, unhappy wife of Alexander II, favoured subdued clothes as far as her position allowed. Her successor, Marie Feodorovna, did not face such marital problems with Alexander III, and she delighted in Worth's gayest creations. Telegrams from St Petersburg were a regular feature of Worth's life, with requests for ball gowns, dinner gowns, day dresses and court official dress whenever Marie Feodorovna had important events coming up on her calendar. She patronized Worth for thirty years, and continued patronizing Jean-Philippe after the great Worth had died.

It was this empress's fervent admiration for Worth's confections which persuaded her sister Alexandra, Princess of Wales, to visit the house, for the two liked to dress alike even though they lived far apart. When a meeting was likely letters flew between them secretly arranging to arrive in identical clothes, and sometimes Worth was involved in the conspiracy. Princess Alexandra, however, was never as regular a patron of the house as her sister, tending to spread her commissions around other Paris and London dressmakers rather than becoming closely associated with one.

The custom of Empress Elizabeth of Austria was undoubtedly a result of Worth's association with Princess Metternich. The high-spirited princess could not stand idly by, seeing the Empress Eugénie being adored in all the elegance of her Worth gowns, without trying to bring such finery to her own mistress. The Empress Elizabeth was younger and more beautiful than the Empress of France, and, as a matter of fact, the Austrians prided themselves that Elizabeth was a proper empress, having been born royal, whereas Eugénie was only the daughter of a count and was really rather fast. Worth's most important order from Empress Elizabeth came when the Austrian Empire was converting itself into the Dual Monarchy of the Austro-Hungarian Empire, in 1867. The empress was a champion of Hungarian rights, while Princess Metternich had a Hungarian count for a father, so here was a dual influence which made Worth decide to design the empress's costume for her coronation with Franz Josef as King and Queen of Hungary, in the Hungarian style. It had a black velvet bodice laced with pearls and a skirt of silver brocade.

The Empress Carlotta of Mexico was a French creation, part of Napoleon III's disastrous attempt to establish a French sphere of influence in the Americas. With French troops and French money supporting this enterprise, it was only natural that the French imperial couturier should do the wardrobe for the new empress, and Carlotta was sent on her tragic mission with her husband, Maximilian of Austria, suitably equipped with quantities

72 The range of couture's clientele: Princess Alexandra of Wales with her sister the future Empress of Russia in identical dresses.

73 The couturier and coronations. Empress Elizabeth of Austria in Charles Frederick Worth's gown for her coronation as Queen of Hungary in 1867. Lithograph by J. Marastori.

74 *Opposite* The continuance of royal custom. Jean-Charles Worth's silver wedding dress for Princess Maria-Mercedes de Bourbon-Orléans.

of Worth evening gowns and day dresses.

As if French, Austrian, Russian and Mexican consorts were not enough, Maison Worth was to receive commissions from an unexpected source, namely Japan. When the Meiji emperor opened that country to the West, not only did he start wearing Western-type uniforms himself, but he expected his empress to adopt Western fashions by obtaining clothes from the house that dressed empresses. Nevertheless there had to be some differences for Japanese ideas of modesty were not the same as those of Europe, so Worth had to create gowns that covered the shoulders because off-the-shoulder evening wear was too sudden a change for Japanese taste.

Sixty years later in the 1920s, Maison Worth was still dressing royalty, even though many kingdoms had fallen by then. When the Pope was upset about the short skirts of the mid-1920s, Jean-Charles Worth designed

Maria de Borbón

Roma - 12 · X · 35 ·

longer skirts as Spanish court dress for Queen Victoria and the Infanta Beatrice in August 1927. That same year Worth's dressed Queen Elizabeth of the Belgians when she attended the wedding of the Duke of Brabant. Indeed royal marriages were a Worth speciality. Also in 1927 Princess Anne of France married Prince Amadeo of Savoy, in Worth's white satin. In 1931 Princess Isabella of Orléans-Bragance wore a Worth gown when she married the Count of Paris. In 1933 Princess Maria-Mercedes of Bourbon-Orléans wore Worth for her marriage to Spain's Prince of Asturias. When King Farouk of Egypt took his first wife, the beautiful Queen Farida, her wedding gown was from the hands of Jean-Charles Worth. The Princess Aga Khan was also a Worth client in the 1930s, and to show that republicans were not ignored, when President Le Brun's son married in 1932 the bride wore a Worth.

Given this sort of clientele it is not surprising that everyone else of note with a wife to dress went to Paris if he could. People with court posts, frequenters of royal circles, members of the diplomatic corps, governors of American states and directors of international companies were just some of the men who clothed their consorts at Maison Worth. It was a question of competition and imitation, of following the example of royalty and striving to be the first to do so. Rather than giving an endless list of such clients, it is simpler to say that there were few who did not frequent that august house in the rue de la Paix.

In addition to these relatively respectable persons from the upper ranks of society whose private lives were not always as virtuous as they liked to pretend, any woman who came into money, either through individual talent such as writing or acting, or through exploiting the lusts of men, was not banned from obtaining her clothes from the imperial couturier. Reputation might be important in the salons, but it was no barrier to be without one as long as one had the money to pay for the creations.

One of these new rich women was the English novelist Ouida. Once her romantic pictures of dashing military heroes in luxurious and exotic settings became best-sellers, allowing the author to take up residence in the Langham Hotel on the proceeds, she started obtaining all her clothes from Worth. She favoured pale colours or white, usually in satin, and liked her fragility to be emphasized by very short sleeves to display her slender arms, and by a skirt raised a little in front to reveal the delicacy of her ankles. To Ouida, a Worth gown became a psychological reinforcement. When she fell in love with the Italian tenor, Mario, at Covent Garden in 1871, a new wardrobe was ordered from Worth to enhance her charms. The clothes might have been fine but even they could not compensate for Ouida's diminutive size, and the ageing tenor was not enraptured. Similarly when she moved to Italy, a wardrobe from Worth was sent for when her Florentine admirer transferred his affections to another lady. When Ouida underwent a rustic phase, there were telegrams to Worth for suitable plain gowns in white muslin, and when in 1886 she decided to revisit England it was with trunkloads of Worths to give her return glamour and style.

A very different set of ladies were those of the ancient profession. The leading courtesans in Paris, several of whom were English, made enormous

75 From the highest to the lowest, couture dressed anyone with the money. Empress Elizabeth of Austria in spangled tulle from Charles Frederick Worth, portrait by Winterhalter.

76 *Opposite* Another Worth
client, the opera star Adelina
Patti, portrait by Sant.

77 Morals no problem;
Edward VII's mistress
Mrs Keppel also dressed
at Worth.

137

sums of money. When Napoleon III dismissed his mistress, Elizabeth Howard, a one-time barmaid in Lambeth, he pensioned her off with the title of countess, a château and an income of £20,000 a year, so that he could marry Eugénie de Montijo. It would have taken an honest labourer five hundred years to earn as much as she was given for one year. With such sums at their disposal, the courtesans spent prodigious amounts on clothes. Society ladies might not admit such women to their houses, but when they went to see Worth they would find them awaiting their turn, for Maison Worth was not an establishment to close the door upon anyone who had the money to buy.

That raucous entertainer of the rich, Cora Pearl, alias Eliza Emma Crouch, spent thousands of pounds at Worth. As she charged 2,000 francs (£80) a night, she could well afford to. With wives supposed to be thoroughly respectable, not to say ignorant of sexual matters beyond child-bearing, wealthy husbands including the emperor himself were happy to pay Cora Pearl's prices for some illicit fun. Good taste was not to be expected of such ladies. The actress-courtesan, Rosalie Léon, was dressed by Worth in lemon taffeta with a dark green sash floating behind. She wore this in her carriage which was lined with violet satin and had grooms in violet liveries. Mme Worth commented that she looked like 'une omelette aux fines herbes'. Such clients, however, could be very loyal, so long as their earning capacity lasted. Mme Musard, *née* Eliza Blakney, was another of Worth's English-born courtesans. She did not make Mlle Léon's mistakes, and had all her carriages upholstered in the colours of her clothes.

Such was the range of clientele in the nineteenth century. The *grandes cocottes* continued shopping at couture houses up to the First World War, but with the collapse of their world their custom ended. New sorts of customers took their place, as the twentieth century got into its stride and the centre of money moved abroad. Royalty of course still came to Paris, as did the aristocracy. In 1938 Paquin could number the Duchess of Windsor, the Duchess of Westminster, the Duchess of Leeds, the Duchess of Villarosa and Baroness Eugénie de Rothschild among its clients, but there was also a new sort of woman buying clothes there, in the person of Marlene Dietrich. The filmstar was the new idealization of glamour, and in the twenties and thirties she was the woman earning the largest sums, apart from the few women heading businesses. The film was an important medium for showing clothes to a wider audience than ever before. The early knock-about comedies did not attempt to be luxurious, but once the cinema started filming plays and stories with upper-class settings, good clothes had to be presented. Couture houses such as Chanel, Paquin and Worth, were called upon to dress the female casts. This gave far-flung audiences, who might never see a wealthy woman with superb clothes in the flesh, the opportunity to witness both the fashions and the luxuries only weeks or months after they were introduced. Not only did this speed up the pace at which fashion was copied, but it increased interest in what the stars wore in their private lives and where they bought their clothes. For the masses, the film-star was the epitome of glamorous fashion far more than any society lady had ever been.

78 This one made no claim to be a lady. Worth's lavish customer, the prostitute Cora Pearl. Her ivy trimmed evening dress and ermine cloak were both ordered by her from Worth to show that she could afford exactly the same clothes as Empress Eugénie.

Not every couture house sought the custom of film-stars. The older houses tended to concentrate on their traditional clientele, and it was a new house, that of Elsa Schiaparelli, that captured much of cinematic custom. Schiaparelli was not afraid of shocking, and liked to play amusing unorthodoxies in her creations, and this was the sort of taste which appealed to a lot of film-stars, whose sophistication was but newly acquired. Joan Crawford adored Schiaparelli's padded shoulders and made them part of her film personality, but she was only one among many. Lauren Bacall, Constance Bennett, Claudette Colbert, Marlene Dietrich, Michele Morgan, Merle Oberon, Norma Shearer, Simone Simon and Gloria Swanson all figured in Schiaparelli's film-world clientele. This set a pattern which was still going strong in 1950 with filmstars sitting next to haute couture's traditional customers, the princesses, duchesses and wives of industrialists, at the spring and autumn collections.

Queen Victoria in 1869 informed the Lord Chancellor of her displeasure at 'the higher classes, in their frivolous, selfish, and pleasure-seeking lives' yet without such lavish expenditure there would have been very little haute couture.

79 *Page 140* A new couture house has a new type of customer: Schiaparelli's filmstar clients, Marlene Dietrich swathed in fox.

80 *Page 141* Constance Bennett, in an evening dress of black and silver.

81 *Page 142* Merle Oberon, in a gown she chose for her private wardrobe.

9 Paris 1914-1939

Whereas Parisian haute couture had been dominated by English and French houses before the Great War, in the post-war period it was to see an increasingly international range of houses, with American, Italian, Spanish and Swiss designers setting up in business as well as new British and French ones. The war itself produced two changes in female dress which would have taken much longer without it. First the war machine devoured so much man-power that women had suddenly to supply the labour in many fields from which they were banned previously. Heavy industry, public transport, agriculture and commerce were just a few of the areas faced with a shortage of men, and women now undertook tasks which a few years before would have been regarded as outside their physical and mental ability. For reasons of patriotism it even became smart for high society ladies to undertake certain forms of work, to help the national cause. Such transformation of the traditional picture of women naturally resulted in sweeping changes in several aspects of their dress. Boiler suits were almost compulsory wear in the munitions industry thus forcing women into trousers, with only the oldest women resisting such practical factory clothing. Knee breeches were

82 Out of fashion and into uniform, which has its compensations by putting a girl alongside more men. Ann Fish, 'Eve works and plays', c. 1916.

83 The softly feminine look for evening to help soldiers forget the war. Paquin's evening gown 'Fuschia', summer 1916.

84 *Opposite* The Spanish look in 1922/3. Sir John Lavery's portrait of his wife Hazel, 'The Silver Swan'.

far better than long skirts for digging in the mud of a wet field. Ankle-length skirts were far more practical for female bus conductors, as were mannish jackets with plenty of pockets. Some women entered the armed forces, and here too their uniforms were closely modelled on the male prototype. All these developments meant that it was now respectable, indeed patriotic, for women to wear trousers and simple, practical clothes, even in the upper reaches of society. Come the peace in 1918, it would not be possible for a couturier to imprison women in highly restrictive clothing again, for those who had become accustomed to easier wear wanted to keep it, and this applied very much to the young.

Fashion itself underwent a major alteration. Whereas the mode before the war had been Poiret's lean line with a high waist, and that lean line was to return by 1917 with a low waist, the years 1915–16 witnessed fashion going out on an unrelated tangent. It did so because there was a new need brought about by the war. The First World War caused the highest rate of casualties in modern history, and the outlook for any young man called up into the army was far from hopeful. The odds were that he would be killed or severely wounded. With such a fate facing sons, brothers and boyfriends, as well as older men, it was imperative that fashion and society should try to compensate. Those men who survived beyond a certain period of the campaign and those who were wounded could escape the horror and come home on leave. Women and dress had to make sure that those troops had a good time and were given everything they might want, before they returned to the trenches and almost certain death. Behaviour was drastically relaxed: if a man held a girl's hand before the war it had been looked upon as a virtual engagement – failure to marry after such a sign of intimacy would have ruined the girl's reputation. The war changed all that. It was now permitted tacitly that a girl might go much further with her boyfriend, be far more loving towards him, for she would probably never see him alive again.

Dress had to change. Men like women with shapely figures – a noticeable bust, a smallish waist, rounded hips, and neat ankles – whatever else fashion might do to them sometimes. Because of the war fashion now produced what soldiers longed for. It brought back feminine shape, but only for the duration of hostilities. Jackets were produced with neat waistlines, skirts were flared out over petticoats, hemlines were raised to show more leg, while evening dresses were cut so low and had such diaphanous bodices that they came close to a naked look. Fashion was responding to a fundamental need: woman as a consolation and refuge.

Once the war was over fashion resumed its original line, which had not been discarded altogether. In fact to begin with there was quite a mixture of influences before the emergence of a very clear line. The exotic East, so beloved of Poiret, was not yet defunct, and turbans, feathers and ropes of jewels lasted into the 1920s. There was a Spanish-South American craze, strongly associated with Valentino as the ideal Latin lover. The discovery of Tut-Ankh-Amun's tomb set off an Egyptian look in 1923. There was a peasant look in 1922, and lastly a medieval influence, stressing low waistlines, hanging sleeves and trailing hems.

Perhaps the most significant alteration in the fashionable ensemble was

85 Clothes in the 1920s were simple in silhouette but complicated in cut. Designs by two of the smaller houses; left, Jane Régny's sports costume of speckled brown and white tweed jersey, with wavy inserts of beige kasha wool jersey; centre, Chantal's golfing frock of wool velours, the jacket of leather brown, the skirt of dark brown with panel of red; right, Chantal's mauve-grey, bordeaux and white tweed with blouse-jacket, and the skirt, with curved panels at the waist, is open at the sides over mauve-grey culottes. André Marty 'Le Départ des Hirondelles', October 1929.

the establishment of a trend that had started before the war, that of the sharp division of the female wardrobe into daytime and evening wear. The elaborate day dress of 1900 and the hobble skirts of 1910 were replaced by very practical garments for the street, for the new woman walked as well as driving. Tailored suits and very simple dresses became the rule for daytime. Exotic outbursts into silks, brocades or velvets were confined more to the evening. Hemlines went through considerable variations before they settled down for a few years. In 1920 both ankle-length and calf-length hems were in fashion, as well as irregular ones with drapery or scarves. By 1922 the trend was back to longer length, and hems hovered above the ankle in 1923–4. It was not until 1925 that skirt hems shot up to just below the knee. It is a length which is associated with the twenties as a whole but it did not appear actually until halfway through that decade.

Who were the couturiers responsible for these many variations and changes? The designers of any one period can be divided into those with a classical, simple taste and those with fussier, more decorative tastes; but any such separation into categories cannot be absolute, for a classicist can become a romantic when the mood is right, although his romanticism may still be less cluttered than that of the romantic proper.

Only one *couturière* had achieved real pominence before the war, Mme Paquin, but after the war no less than five women designers were making names for themselves. Foremost among these in impact was Coco Chanel. Gabrielle Chanel, as was her real name, had been born in 1883 and had an unhappy childhood from which she emerged as a rather tomboyish character, fond of riding and wearing men's breeches and hacking jackets. When she was twenty-seven she was in the midst of a great love affair with the Englishman Boy Capel, who made a fortune out of coal. It was he who showed her Parisian high life and took her round the social circuit. Her sense of fashion began to emerge at this point. Having worn simple clothes hitherto, she was not interested in the showy dresses of 1910–14, nor did she care for the over-decorated hats. She bought hats from Galerie Lafayette and removed the trimmings, wearing the very plain results about town. Many ladies expressed their admiration, and eventually Chanel decided that if these women did not have the intelligence to make such hats themselves by doing what she did, then she would open a hat shop and make them pay for her ideas. Her lover provided the financial backing and set Chanel up with a hat shop in the fashionable resort of Deauville. This proved very successful, and by 1912 her hats were in the fashion magazines.

Chanel did not lose her fondness for wearing masculine garments when she thought they felt right. One cold day in 1914 she put on a man's sweater; Boy Capel and his English polo friends passed no comment, but French women were quite impressed. It was a daring idea but so practical for the seaside; and Chanel found that her hat shop had now to stock men's sweaters as well. The same thing happened when she wore a straight marine's jacket on the promenade; other women wanted it. This determined Chanel to open a dress shop in Paris, but the First World War broke out and ruined her chances. After the war, in 1919, Chanel reopened as a couture house, although this was the blackest time for her emotionally as Capel, married to someone else but still a close friend, was killed in a car crash. Chanel buried herself in work, and applied the same attitude to clothes that had made such an impact in Deauville, which became the philosophy of her house. Clothes must be casual and easy to wear. Her creations were the acme of simplicity, plain sweaters over pleated skirts with easy jackets – relaxed, rather boyish clothing without clutter.

The clothes of Coco Chanel were common sense. Her feeling was for the mathematical and the practical, so garments had to work. Pockets must be practical pockets in sensible places, and buttons must button, not be mere decoration. Chanel stripped off the inessential and the showy, refining the line and replacing the over-dressed woman with the understated lady. She made it chic to look poverty-stricken, cutting clothes down to the bare essentials, and only then allowing some inexpensive ornamentation in the form of costume jewellery – not real gems. There were some proud names who had become poor, and Chanel's style was highly apposite to them. Russian grandees had to work as taxi-drivers, and grand duchesses as models. Chanel herself went out with the poverty-stricken Grand Duke Dimitri, so she could see their problems at first hand. Her clothes were an expression of reality.

Chanel took a lot of inspiration from menswear and the working class. In addition to sweaters, she used stonemasons' neckerchiefs and mechanics' dungarees, converting them into luxurious simplicity. She took sailors' bell-bottoms and made them smart for women, particularly at the seaside, saying that she was tired of seeing people sitting around in wet bathing costumes. A devotee of fresh air and sunshine, she had never minded getting sunburnt when young, and her suntans in the twenties revolutionized the

86 Coco Chanel in one of her own suits in 1929, soft easy jersey wool, with one of her sleeveless jumpers, as simple as could be.

attitude of society. A suntan became smart. Instead of wintering in the South of France as had been the custom started by the English aristocracy, the young started going there in the summer and abandoning their parasols.

Chanel was the ideal of her own fashion: she designed for herself and other women copied. During her tremendous success in the 1920s and 1930s she was actually in her forties and fifties, but she made it possible for the older woman to look young. She dressed rather like a schoolgirl, with a white blouse and a dark blue suit, but by avoiding any fussiness she made the result the acme of sophistication.

It is rather symptomatic of women couturiers to create clothes on the body instead of by making sketches. Chanel was no exception, and very

rarely drew a design. Because of this, she never created uncomfortable clothes. Lamé was irritating next to the skin, so she did not put it there. Tight clothes were ugly as well as inconvenient, so she concentrated on easy fit. No sewer herself, she was very handy with the scissors and would not hesitate to pull a garment apart if she felt it to be even slightly awkward. In a word, she loosened everything up.[1]

In complete contrast to the restrained Chanel was the Italian Elsa Schiaparelli (1890–1972). The daughter of a Roman professor, she had married a Pole and lived in America before getting divorced and ending up in Paris very poor. It was in 1927 that she made her entry into fashion. She had knitted herself a black sweater with a *trompe l'oeil* white bow and collar as part of the garment. A buyer saw her in it and promptly ordered some copies, so Schiaparelli had to rush about and organize herself into a business, without any idea of how to proceed. Luckily she found some refugee Armenian women who could knit well, and she engaged them to

87 Chanel was her own ideal, illustrating her philosophy by what she wore, for her clothes and her concepts were one. An absolutely plain black dress with lots of costume jewellery, and her hair tied with ribbon like a little girl.

88 The first Schiaparelli, a *trompe l'oeil* sweater in black and white wool, 1927.

produce copies of her sweater. She took a garret in the fashionable rue de la Paix and set up as a sweater designer to begin with, for her own sweater had made the pages of *Vogue* and other orders were coming in.

Schiaparelli made *trompe l'oeil* effects a speciality, creating sweaters with African designs, tattoo patterns, and X-ray ribs, and swimming suits with pictures of fish on them. She concentrated on casual and sportswear to start with and only gradually moved into the more luxurious area of evening wear. She made her impact as the joker in the world of fashion, and applied the same comic effects to dresses as to sweaters. She teamed a jacket with an evening dress, which seemed a very strange notion at first but which proved very elegant and effective in a black sheath of crêpe de chine with a jacket in white, an ideal ensemble for dining out. In 1933 Schiaparelli hit the headlines with her pagoda sleeve, or Egyptian look. She enlarged the head of the sleeve to form a big epaulette and suddenly fashion acquired a new highlight. Women were to have wide shoulders for the next fourteen years. Her intention was to make waists look smaller by padding out the sleeves at the top, but she felt that many of those who copied her idea went too far, exaggerating the sleeve too much. Such a person was the Hollywood film costumier, Adrian, who was over-enthusiastic in his reaction, producing monstrous sleeves for the stars, which Schiaparelli thought *de trop*.

Elsa Schiaparelli was not a sophisticated designer in the sense that her clothes were a continuous evolution, nor did she have a great feeling for cloth; she was much more the witty entertainer, sparkling with startling novelties. She brought a sense of fun to fashion, and travelled far and wide in search of ideas for clothes. From the Alps she brought Swiss sweaters and the Tyrolean look, from India saris, from Peru bright patterns. After seeing old women in the Copenhagen fish market wearing newspaper hats, she had a fabric made with a newspaper print which she used for scarves, blouses and hats. This was a typical Schiaparelli skill – converting something ordinary into a witty item of high fashion, and can be compared with Chanel's use of artisans' clothes. Not surprisingly the two designers did not get on together. Chanel did not regard Schiaparelli as a couturier, but rather as a brazen Italian interloper who made dresses. Schiaparelli stole the headlines in the 1930s, for journalists loved her clever tricks, but Chanel was too well established by then for it to damage her bank balance.

1935 was an important year for Schiaparelli. She acquired much larger premises at 21 Place Vendôme where she opened one of the first couture boutiques, selling sweaters, skirts and blouses ready-made instead of the usual bespoke. Her collections that year were alive with her fantastic devilry – tweed for evening, padlock fasteners on suits, and evening raincoats. She made zips high fashion by using them as decorations in coloured plastic from ICI. Zips were not new by any means, dating back to the previous century, and were widely used on luggage. Gorin was the first house in Paris to use them in spring 1930, but had concealed them under ruching. Schiaparelli made zips obvious. Bravado was her style.

In 1938 she used two themes for inspiration. From astrology she took planets, stars and the animals of the zodiac, embroidering them on evening jackets; and she did the same thing with the circus, producing balloon

handbags and ice-cream cone hats. These comic hats were one of her special lines, and she designed the shoe-shape hat and the lamb-cutlet hat, which her client, Mrs Fellowes, wore with great flair. Another of her customers was Mrs Wallis Simpson who ordered eighteen frocks from Schiaparelli just before her marriage to the Duke of Windsor.

To assist in her search for novelty, Schiaparelli turned to contemporary artists. The Surrealist movement had begun in the early twenties and its use of fantasy and unexpected juxtaposition had made a great impact on Schiaparelli. What she did was to introduce such ideas into fashion, and to ask the artists themselves to co-operate. Salvador Dali helped her to translate his picture of a woman made of drawers into a coat with drawers down the front. In 1937 Jean Cocteau drew a design of a face and hands which she had embroidered on a grey linen evening suit and on a coat; and Christian Bérard designed a Medusa head which she had embroidered on the back of a cape. Not for nothing did Schiaparelli name her house perfume 'Shocking'; it summed up her whole approach of elegant outrage.[2]

Older than both Chanel and Schiaparelli was Jeanne Lanvin (1867–1946). She had been trained as a dressmaker back in the nineteenth century, and then worked as a milliner. She had used her skills to make children's clothes, first for her little sister and subsequently for her own daughter. These were so admired by others that she began to make them on a commercial basis, and as her daughter grew up she altered her enterprise into a couture house, just before the First World War. Clothes for mother and daughter in matching ensembles became her distinctive sphere. Lanvin was fifty-one when the First World War ended, hardly an age to join in any revolutionary trends in fashion. During the 1920s and 1930s she represented the survival of romantic clothes, in a period of chromium plating and casual dress. Jeanne Lanvin did not abandon the full skirts of 1915–16 but used them for years afterwards in what were known as her picture frocks. When waistlines slid down to hip level, she adjusted the fullness to flair from the hip, but that was her only concession to modernity in skirts. It might be the era of motor cars and aeroplanes, but there was at the same time a nostalgia for things past. Mock-Tudor flourished in British suburbs, and Liberty's had a whole wing rebuilt in Tudor style. For this mood Lanvin's picture frocks were ideal. It was highly appropriate that Lanvin's favourite customer was the singer, Yvonne Printemps, for she was a star of musical comedy, where romantic clothes thrived. By wearing Lanvin's picture frocks off-stage, Printemps was a splendid advertisement of the style. She also loved Lanvin's luxurious furs.

Lanvin's most startling innovation had been at the beginning of the war, when she had devised her chemise dress. In construction it was as simple as a sack, and was probably inspired by the simplicity of Poiret's creations. Being so easy to make, especially for those who could not afford to go to dressmakers, it became a great success with the young and was a prototype of the straight-up-and-down dresses of the twenties. Lanvin herself retained something of the exoticism of the pre-war period, wearing Chinese quilted jackets and outré jewellery, and using rich oriental fabrics for evening. There was nothing old-fashioned however about her gifts for

89 Schiaparelli's pagoda sleeves, emphasizing the shoulders in order to minimize the waist; these examples were available from Harrods. Drawing by Eric, March 1933.

LA FÊTE EST FINIE

Robe d'organdi et robe de petite fille, de Jeanne Lanvin

90 Keeping the full skirt alive, regardless of what other couturiers did. Jeanne Lanvin's organdi matching ensembles for mother and daughter at garden parties. Drawing by Pierre Brissaud, May 1920.

organization and management, for Jeanne Lanvin built her business up into a major enterprise. Although not in the forefront of fashion, she maintained a steady growth and was willing to diversify. In 1926 she opened the first boutique for men, to run alongside her couture and children's wear. Her organizational abilities were recognized in 1937 when she was made president of the haute couture committee for the Paris International Exhibition, when she was seventy. In 1939 she was the Paris representative at the New York World's Fair. Such was her efficiency that she created a house which could carry on after her own demise.[3]

Madeleine Vionnet was very different. Her house was so much herself that it could only last as long as she did, for she was an individual artist and not an organizer. Born in 1876, she had a long career as a seamstress before becoming a couturier. At twelve her father had apprenticed her to a Paris dressmaker, and at sixteen she graduated to the dressmaker, Vincent, in the rue de la Paix. After an unsuccessful marriage when she was eighteen, she went to London for five years, where she was put in charge of a tailor's workroom with twelve men under her control. In 1901 she returned to Paris and became *toile*-maker to Mme Gerber, the main designing member of Callot Soeurs, whom Vionnet considered a better creator than Poiret. It was her job to work out designs in thin linen, realizing a dress, and to produce copies of this master *toile* for sale to buyers. After two years there she moved to Doucet for five years where, as we have seen, she claimed to have discarded corsets before Poiret. When she was over thirty Vionnet opened her own couture business but, like Chanel, she was forced to close down by the First World War. In 1922 she was offered the lease on a mansion in the Avenue Montaigne, and re-opened her couture house there.

By spring 1924 the fashion press was reporting what was to be the outstanding characteristic of Vionnet, her beautiful feeling for drapery. She presented evening dresses in crêpe with a novel system of draping the skirt to one side in front and catching it by fine shirring. Many of her frocks had a Grecian simplicity, finely pleated and held by cords. Like Chanel, Vionnet did not sketch; she created on the body. From her past work with *toiles* she

91 *Left* An early design by Madeleine Vionnet, a wrap-over coat in bouclé wool, with contrasting collar and cuffs, 1924–5.

92 *Right Prima inter pares.* Madeleine Vionnet as queen of the couturiers, hailed by *Harper's* as the goddess of the bias cut and greatest of them all, November 1934.

LA VITRINE

MANTEAU, DE MADELEINE VIONNET

Modèle déposé. Reproduction interdite.

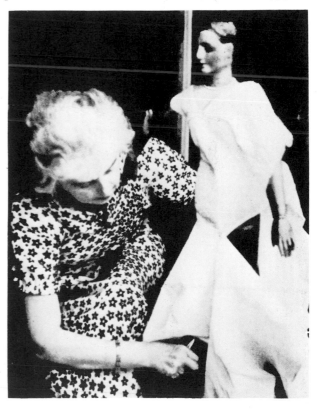

was able to use fabric and cut more brilliantly than any one else in the business at that date. She had been called the inventor of the bias cut, which is rather a sweeping statement considering the thousands of years when clothes have been worn and bias could have been used either by accident or design. Nevertheless she made the construction of clothes on the bias a fundamental part of her house policy, and she became famous for it.

Cloth cut on the bias forms a very fluid line. It responds to and reflects every undulation of the body, and subtly discloses the rhythms of feminine shape. The women who went to Vionnet had to have good figures, for there was no padding, no disguising, no covering of bodily faults by artifice. Her dresses took the shape of the wearers, which gave them a magical quality. They flowed on the person with great ease, mirroring every movement or change of stance. They did so because Vionnet created them in the round. First of all she would try out an idea on a figurine, carefully smoothing the material and applying her scissors until she had worked out the most satisfactory solution. Not until this process was perfect would she go on to produce a pattern for a full-scale dress. In the opinion of the president of the Chambre Syndicale, Jacques Worth, she was the best technician in all couture. It was from this play with fabrics that Vionnet evolved the halter and cowl necklines, both reflecting the nature of textiles themselves.

It was because her approach was so personal that Vionnet preferred to work for individual women. The Queen of the Belgians, the Rothschilds, Mme Clemenceau and Mme Citroën were her clientele. She did not like the idea of creating dresses to be copied by foreign buyers for anonymous women whom she would never see. For the sake of business she had to accept foreign orders, but her heart was not in it. In 1931 her satin evening dresses were a hot favourite with Americans, while 1933 was hailed as the year of her supreme collection, with floating draperies flaring at the back of evening gowns, and stiffened folds like terraces. She invented a coat which fastened at the back, but this was a piece of humour too difficult to live with. Two weeks before her autumn show in 1934 she sensed that romanticism was in the air and scrapped her collection, working feverishly to devise a more nineteenth-century feel. She showed, on time, gowns in taffeta and velvet with bustle effects, and picture gowns with full bell skirts. The style that Jeanne Lanvin had adhered to was coming back into fashion.

Although she avoided personal publicity, the trade looked upon Vionnet as an immortal ideal. When the lease on her couture house ran out in 1940 she decided to retire after a legal row with her sleeping partner, and she was widely acknowledged as the greatest artist in fabrics, a supreme master of subtle construction whom no other could rival. When she died in 1975, just short of her centenary, respect for her work had not diminished.[4]

Last among the great female designers of the inter-war years is Mme Grès. As a girl in the 1920s she wanted to be a sculptor, but her family was horrified at the thought of a girl wanting to be an artist. Unwilling to give up her ambition, Grès sought another way to sculpt, and turned to fabrics. She experimented by making *toiles*, and found that couture houses were willing to buy them. Encouraged by this she opened her own shop in 1930, after only three months' training in cutting. For her it was the material which

determined how she could make a dress, and this gave her the confidence to start. She went into business as Alix Barton, and found that her loose coats sold very well. This was a mixed blessing, because she had no business experience to cope with expanding orders. By 1934 she decided that she would be better off working for an established house, and joined the firm of Alix as designer. For this reason her creations for the rest of the 1930s were known as Alix.

As Vionnet had made the bias cut all the rage, Grès turned her attention to the possibilities of drapery on the straight. Being a sculptor by instinct she had a great feeling for classical Greek sculpture, and sought to recapture some of its timeless elegance in her clothes. She created dresses which looked simple but which were the result of hours of pleating and draping. Like Vionnet, Grès created on the living body, and her models had to possess immense patience, posing for a whole day, as she pinned and folded the fabric. Wool jersey was a stuff which pleated beautifully, so it became a mainstay of her style, allowing for the play of light and shade in its deep folds. Typical of her creations was an evening gown in black jersey in 1935. The pleats were formed by a drawstring at the neck and fell straight down to

93 *Left* Vionnet in classic mood, a Directoire line sheath with swathed bodice in lime yellow crêpe, worn with a hooded cape in black Chantilly lace, from Jacqmar, March 1937, photo by Horst.

94 *Right* Vionnet in romantic mood, white organza dress with Victorian-size skirt and black velvet sash round a wasp waist, with a black Chantilly lace coat, March 1937, photo by Horst.

95 *Left* Alix, sculptural folds in a gown of black jersey with cartridge pleated sleeves like folded wings, February 1935, drawing by Reynaldo Luza.

96 *Right* Alix: statuesque beauty that can never date, 1937, photo by Man Ray.

the feet, being gathered also at the waist by a silver belt. It was featured in *Harper's Bazaar*, for Grès attained instant success when she was at Alix. Another of her classical gowns, in white jersey, which appeared in that magazine in 1937, became a timeless epitome of elegance in a dateless photograph.

In 1942 during the German occupation, Grès decided to open as a couturier again, now that she had plenty of experience. Unfortunately the Germans closed her down for a period because she had dared to design in patriotic red, white and blue. She named her own house Grès, as this was the name used by her husband Serge Czerefkov when signing his paintings. There were never any assistant designers at Grès. Like Vionnet, she created all her own *toiles*, which her staff then made out as patterns. Unlike other couturiers she kept her presentations extremely simple. The models did not wear jewels, accessories or gloves, for only the dress mattered. Nothing, said Madame, must detract from that.[5]

Chanel, Vionnet and Grès may all be regarded as classic designers, with Lanvin as the romantic and Schiaparelli as the shocker. This pattern can also be seen among the males. There were a great many couturiers in Paris in the twenties and thirties, more than in the previous decades, although none of them became such a legend as Chanel. They were so numerous, in fact, that it is not possible to treat them all with equal justice.

At the oldest couture house, Jean-Charles Worth was now the chief designer, for Jean-Philippe had retired after the war, dying in 1926. Gaston the administrator had died in 1924, so Jacques Worth was in charge of that department, and he was so efficient an administrator that he became president of the Chambre Syndicale de la Haute Couture twice, in 1927–30 and 1933–35, as well as being vice-president of the Syndicat des Tissus. His medical training was not abandoned completely, for he was also treasurer of the League against Cancer, and founder of a Franco-American charity for children with tuberculosis.

Jean-Charles Worth tends to be forgotten today, but he was hailed as a great designer by the fashion press of the day. The *Paris Times* described him in 1927 as 'tall, gracious, in manner, a linguist. He is an artist to his finger-tips, yet one who seems reluctant to speak too much of his striking talents.' His collection of 1923 had dark velvet as its keynote for even the simplest dresses. An innovation he made in evening wear was to insert a narrow panel into one side of his very long, slender gowns, by way of contrast. He used diamond studs as a novel trimming. Two of his ideas of May 1927 attracted considerable press comment. The hip-level waistline having been fashionable now for several years, he started a move back towards the natural waist by introducing his slanting waistline, which began at hip level at the back but which rose to natural level in front. He also dropped the hemlines of evening dresses, which had become as short as day wear in the mid-twenties, thereby initiating a trend which other couturiers soon followed. When interviewed by *Liberty* at that date he stated: 'Creating clothes is, like architecture, a matter of good proportion and design and harmony. Anything in its place is beautiful; outside of its place it is ugly.' The ideal of contemporary fashion, as he saw it, was casual richness: 'It is

97 *Left* The trend back to the normal waist and lowering the hemline; Jean-Charles Worth's suit 'Suivez-Moi' with check blouse, worn by his house model Anita, 1928.

98 *Right* Jean-Charles Worth's summer suit 'Etincelle' with abstract print silk blouse, worn by house model Renée, May 1929.

99 *Left* One of Jean-Charles Worth's best sellers in 1927, a knitted evening dress worn by house model Maroussia, and named 'Tabac Blond'.

100 *Right* One of Jean-Charles Worth's customers: Mme Dubonnet in his white satin evening dress 'Oui ou Non', 1928.

101 *Left* Mme Gulbenkian in Jean-Charles Worth's British court dress, May 1929.

102 *Right* The Princess of Montenegro in a Jean-Charles Worth evening dress of a white print on black with clusters of brilliants on the chest. Called 'Pleine d'Audace', this model was withdrawn once it had been sold to a royal client, so that no copies were available

103 Jean-Charles Worth's
pyjama evening suits; left,
gold lamé interwoven with
multicoloured flowers; right,
white trousers and top, with
blue jacket, 1930.

youthful, and today all women are young.' This epitomizes the great change that had taken place in fashion. Mothers and daughters now dressed much the same; there was none of the sharp division of simple frocks for girls and lavish gowns for older women which had characterized the pre-war period. One illustration of the new casual wear was Worth's pyjama evening suit which he launched in 1930, the sort of garment that would have been unthinkable in his youth.

In addition to all the royal clientele it still had, the house continued to dress the aristocracy and the stage. Baroness de Stoeckl called in 1921, her first visit since 1913, owing to the war. As a matter of fact there was an outstanding bill for 2,500 francs; Jacques Worth said nothing during the baroness's visit, but next morning that bill was delivered to her hotel without fail. Much larger bills were run up by the actress, Ida Rubenstein, who had been a customer since at least 1913. In 1920, when she was to act Cleopatra, she ordered the costumes from Maison Worth at a cost of 15,000 to 20,000 francs each. Another wealthy client at this time was Lady Mountbatten, one of the leaders of the twenties' social scene, with an income of £45,000 a year. When she sailed for Malta in 1927 she took a whole wardrobe of Worth gowns in satin and lamé. Thus when Jean-Charles retired in 1935 he could claim that he had not allowed the status of the house to decline. He did not die until 1962, at eighty-one. As Jean-Charles' children were not considered suitable to take his place as designer, it was Roger Worth, eldest of Jacques Worth's three sons, who was appointed at the age of twenty-seven. The firm now moved from its home in the rue de la Paix, where it had been for seventy-seven years, to premises in the Faubourg St Honoré. The London branch was made into a separate business with Elspeth Champcommunal as its designer since her own little couture business had earlier collapsed, during the slump. The London branch was to remain as a privileged customer of the Paris house[6] (see chapter 10).

In contrast to the established houses, there were a great many new ones opening up in the inter-war period. Jean Patou was one of the more important newcomers. He had tried to become a couturier before the war, when he used to have a small dressmaker's called Parry, and was greatly encouraged when a New York retailer bought his entire collection. Thinking it might be possible to upgrade his business to couture, Patou was preparing a couture collection in 1914 when the war broke out. Like Chanel and Vionnet he did not seem to notice that the war was coming. Patou then spent four years as a captain of Zouaves, before returning to open as a couturier proper in 1919. Sportswear was an important part of his creation, and the leading tennis star Suzanne Lenglen was dressed by him in extremely simple tunic tops and pleated skirts which caused a revolution in the world of sport. His philosophy of design was akin to Chanel's in stripping a dress down to its cleanest line, and he saw that great *couturière* as his bitterest enemy, and rival. Like could not tolerate like, it seems. Perhaps Patou was rather vain; certainly he was considered a tall, dark, handsome fellow by the ladies, and he was jealous of Chanel stealing any of the limelight, which he wished to monopolize.

Patou enjoyed his greatest success in 1929. In the spring collections he

showed the princess line, the dress moulded from a high waist, thereby marking the end of the hip level waist. In the autumn he took a tremendous risk over hemlines. Skirts had been very short for only four years, but Patou did not like them. When a lady sat down it meant quite a display of stocking tops, suspenders and undies, which was very untidy to say the least. As Patou said in an interview in *La Liberté*, short skirts were simply not haute couture, and were essentially vulgar. So he dropped the hemline to below the calf. It had a phenomenal success and was the sort of fashion which manufacturers detested, for it made every dress in stock out of date overnight. Patou died young in 1936 but his house was continued by his brother-in-law Raymond Barbas, who was to recruit Marc Bohan as designer.[7]

Perhaps the master of subtle innovation in fashion was Captain Edward Molyneux to whom the shock treatment of Patou's dropped hems was rather bad form. Molyneux had begun as a designer before the war, for Lucile had placed him in her Paris branch when she opened it in 1911. Indeed, in later years, she rarely failed to mention that she had trained the great Molyneux. During the war Molyneux served in the British Army and emerged with the

104 *Left* Jean Patou designs for dining. Seated, a black crêpe skirt and jacket of black paillettes, with little hat of black paillettes and paradise fronds. Standing, black crêpe gown with crisp white piqué collar and cuffs, February 1935.

105 *Right* Patou: black crêpe, diagonally pleated across the body and ending in a ruffle on the shoulder, pleated pale pink sash, hat by Rose Valois in black crêpe trimmed with pink wax flowers. Intricacy that could only be seen close up, July 1937.

SHOWING UNERRING APPRECIATION OF STATUESQUE LINES AND COLOUR HARMONIES

FROCKS OF EXTREME SIMPLICITY CARRIED OUT IN UNUSUALLY INTERESTING FABRICS.

106 Molyneux's trousseau for the Duchess of Kent; 1 black cloqué satin evening dress slit in the skirt to reveal silver lamé. 2 black velvet evening gown with natural pigskin belt and gloves. 3 evening dress in bois de rose crêpe façonné with loose coat in beige velvet lined with the same crêpe. 4 afternoon ensemble in heavy crinkly crêpe with matching coat trimmed with fox. 5 black woollen coat with calf leather belt, and astrakhan collar. 6 morning ensemble, in almond-green trimmed with nutria, the dress is shown separately on the far right as 6A. 7 black crêpe afternoon frock with loose sleeves ending in fringes, and a necktie of orange velvet. Drawings by Evelyne Norris, December 1934.

rank of captain, proudly retaining that title thereafter. In 1919 he opened his own house in Paris and his understated clothes were to become classics of the next three decades. Molyneux's was a very British establishment. When young Balmain joined it as junior designer in 1934, the secretary, John Cavanagh, was British and so was the *directrice*, and a thoroughly British upper-class restraint characterized the clothes which originated there. These were dresses and suits for ladies who liked to be well dressed without attracting comment. Everything was discreet, every change was subtle. These were clothes for connoisseurs.

Molyneux was, in the eyes of the next generation of designers, the master whom they revered. Balmain was deeply impressed by the belief in simplicity, by the avoidance of gaudy detail, by the fondness for beige, a muted tone which sums up Molyneux's whole attitude. Christian Dior was to prefer Molyneux to any other couturier, for nothing was ever invented for the sake of novelty, but evolved very smoothly from the preceding style. Molyneux was an ideal classicist whom others could but aspire to equal.

An example of the subtle nature of Molyneux's innovations can be seen in his Eastern look for 1934. This consisted of such details as bamboo buttons on a navy suit and a little hat of bamboo-yellow straw. That was all: there were no lurid kimonos or Chinese hairpins, but just enough to give fashion reporters something to write about, the suggestion of a theme. That same spring, and at the same time as Worth, Molyneux introduced loose, long jackets for suits, in natural linen, to be worn with blouses of silk, crepe or organdie. It does not follow that Molyneux's clothes lacked colour. To enliven the little black dress he introduced three-quarter length coats in bright yellow wool or white linen. Similarly for evening in 1935 he put a white piqué cape over a black gown. From 1935 Molyneux was gradually shortening skirts from the calf length set by Patou. In 1936 he did mess jackets with pleated skirts cut on the cross, and for autumn, suits in Scottish plaid, with fitted jackets and slightly flared skirts, reaching just below the knee. His skirts were never too long nor too short, whatever other couturiers might do.

Classic master though he was, Molyneux did not ignore the romantic trend. In 1937 he showed a picture gown in black tulle, the skirt flared out over a crinoline like a Winterhalter portrait of the Second Empire. The romantic look back at the nineteenth century was never perfect – such revivals never are – and it mixed bustles of the 1880s, crinolines of the 1850s and hairstyles upswept in the Edwardian manner. But even here, Molyneux was discreet.

His clientele were women for whom good taste mattered more than show. Gertrude Lawrence he dressed for nothing, for so famous a star was his advertisement. Her Molyneux wardrobe for the role of Amanda in Noël Coward's *Private Lives* in 1930 made women drool with envy. When the play moved to New York early in 1931, Molyneux sent a new wardrobe exactly the same as the old, after six weeks, so that the clothes always appeared fresh on stage.

Molyneux's most elegant client was a Greek princess by the name of Marina. She was already a customer at Maison Molyneux when she became betrothed to the Duke of Kent. This engagement sparked off fierce rivalry between couture houses in both London and Paris in 1934. The British dressmakers said they should have the honour of making the wedding dress, as they were the traditional dressmakers to the British royal family. The Paris houses contested that the glory of such an order ought to come to them, as they were long used to dressing royal brides. An additional

107 Molyneux's mistake. Left, Queen Mary in a face-revealing toque, the Duchess of Kent hidden by Molyneux's cartwheel hat, the Duke of Kent, and far right the Duchess of York in a face-revealing cloche hat, May 1935.

108 *Left* Princess Natalie Paley dressed by her husband Lucien Lelong in a grey cloth coat, trimmed with fox o a grey-beige crêpe frock, pleated across the body from r to left, 1928.

109 *Above* A Lelong travel coat in green homespun, do breasted for warmth, with flat grey astrakhan collar and shoulder pieces; a Lelong coat-frock in very dark brown angora jersey trimmed with yellow broadcloth, white an belt with brown and yellow buckle, March 1932.

complication was the plea from the impoverished Russian refugees in Paris, asking for some of the work for themselves, as the princess's mother had been a Russian grand duchess. Such demands required very diplomatic handling from Princess Marina, and her decision was a compromise. She would get her wedding dress from her Parisian couturier, Molyneux, who was British anyway; as many British materials as possible would be used in its making, and some of the work should be given to the Russian refugees. That settled the matter, and the wedding in November 1934 showed Molyneux's elegance to the world.[8]

Next year Molyneux had to dress the new Duchess of Kent for another major event, the silver jubilee of King George V in May 1935. He designed a dress and jacket in pale grey, the sleeves edged with fur. The costume was so simple that it defied description. There was nothing about it to cause comment, but it was the height of sophistication and the epitome of Molyneux's style. What did cause comment was the duchess's hat. This was one of Molyneux's elegant cartwheels, in grey and trimmed with grey feathers, which the duchess wore in the angled manner of the thirties. It completed the ensemble perfectly but it concealed part of the duchess's face as she drove in an open carriage through London, and it was a rule of British monarchy that the royal face should always be clearly visible to all the public. The duchess and Molyneux did not make that mistake again.

Lucien Lelong opened his couture house in 1923. He was an example of the couturier who could make clothes but who had no talent for design. He gained a reputation for excellent workmanship, and employed young designers to create ideas. Lelong married Princess Natalie Paley, daughter of Grand Duke Paul of Russia, and the clothes he made for her gave her the reputation as one of the best dressed women in Paris. The style of his house was the casual elegance so typical of the day, and often appeared in *Vogue* and *Harper's Bazaar* in the 1920s and 1930s. By the end of the period Lelong's house was in decline. Balmain, who went there as designer in 1939, felt that Lelong was a dealer in dresses, doing limited editions of ready-to-wear for the provinces and French Africa, rather than a true couturier. Nevertheless Lelong was elected president of the Chambre Syndicale from 1937 to 1945, and he deserves high honour for what he was to do to save French couture during the war.

Marcel Rochas, who was born in Paris, opened in 1925 at 14 avenue Matignon. He was full of ideas for fashions, and would fiercely dispute with other couturiers if it was said that they had had an idea before he did. For example, he contested Schiaparelli's large shoulder fashion of 1933, saying that he had seen similar exaggerated shoulders on Javanese and Balinese dancers at the Exposition Coloniale in 1931 and had introduced them to fashion then. The press took the view that the honours were shared equally between the two houses. In 1930 there was a sensation when no less than eight women at a party found themselves wearing an identical Rochas model. This showed great carelessness on Rochas's part. It would be all right to sell the same dress to women widely scattered abroad, but to have done so in Paris, where each dress was supposed to be a unique creation for which the customer had paid dear, was the height of folly. The wise couturier kept records of sales

The new definition of "Dressy"

110 The tunic afternoon dress. Left, by Lanvin in black velvet with modified melon sleeves and detachable quilted scarf; right, Mainbocher's longer tunic, with very square shoulders and a high Edwardian neckline in fine black wool, a superb background for ropes of pearls, October 1934.

to ensure that such accidents could not occur.

The American in Parisian couture was Main Rousseau Bocher. Born in Chicago in 1890, he had studied art in New York, Paris and Munich, supplementing his income by doing some fashion sketching. After the First World War he remained in Paris to study singing. To help his finances he took some sketches to Molyneux, where he did not make a sale but was told that *Harper's* was looking for an illustrator. He got the job at 100 dollars a week, intending to carry on with his singing as well, but his voice failed and he was forced to make sketching his career. *Vogue* snapped him up in 1922 (which was typical of the warfare between the two leading fashion magazines), where he rose to become Paris fashion editor and then editor of the whole French issue. In 1929 he decided that after watching other people's fashion ideas for so long, he would show that he had some of his own. He set up his own house, merging his name into Mainbocher. As he

111 Mainbocher simplicity, a boxy jacket in grey men's suiting over a bias cut dress, March 1937.

was so well known in the fashion press he had a terrific advantage over any other couturier trying to make himself known for the first time.

Mainbocher's style reflected the classicism of Chanel and Molyneux in its avoidance of fuss. His view was 'don't dress up; dress down.' This can be seen in the clothes he designed for the Duchess of Windsor in 1936/7, for being a fellow American she gave him a lot of encouragement. From classicism Mainbocher went over to romanticism in the late thirties, introducing in 1939 the small waist which was laced in like a Victorian corset, and such nineteenth-century fabrics as embroidered satin. The outbreak of the Second World War, however, froze this fashion development, and Mainbocher went back home to the United States. He opened a couture house at West 57th Street in New York, with the ultimate intention of returning to Paris after the war. In the event he did so well that he stayed in America.[9]

Robert Piguet, a Swiss, was working for Redfern in the early thirties but he opened his own house at rue du Cirque in the middle of that decade. Like Lelong he was a dressmaker who did not design but who was good at making clothes. He purchased designs, and in 1933 and 1937 he bought sketches from young Balmain and then from Dior. In 1938 he engaged Dior as his full-time designer and moved to the Round Point des Champs Elysées. Piguet participated in the romantic revival, producing day dresses with Edwardian necklines and full skirts, but when the war came he had to return to Switzerland for military duty and he faded from the fashion scene.

Two important houses were founded just before the war. Jacques Fath opened his in 1937. He had been trained in a business school and at a drama school, but at twenty-five he turned to dressmaking. The influence that led him to do so can be seen in his family background; his father was an artist and his great-grandmother, whom he liked to talk to when young, had been a dressmaker under the Second Empire. His collection in 1937 was only about twenty dresses, but from such small beginnings he rose very rapidly and was listed among the more important couturiers by the time the war came.

Cristobal Balenciaga was born in the Basque region of Spain in 1895. As a child he liked sewing, and the story has it that the local *marquessa* allowed him to copy her suit from Drécoll of Paris. After this lesson he studied tailoring, and when a young man opened his own little dressmaking shop in San Sebastian. He managed to go to Paris once to see the collections, and resolved to set himself up there one day. He saved up hard, and when the Spanish Civil War broke out in 1936 Balenciaga decided that the time had come to move to Paris. His clothes had a dramatic simplicity, stemming from the tailored line and the absence of unnecessary detail. *Harper's Bazaar* featured him in 1937, and by the time of the war he was successfully launched as a Parisian couturier.

IO Developments in London

Whereas native British talent in dress design had tended to gravitate to Paris before 1900, if it wanted to succeed at the highest international level, by the turn of the century that talent was keener on making London the principal rival to Paris. While Worth and Redfern had branches in both cities, the first couture house of international importance to make London its main base was that of Lucile.

Lucy Kennedy was born about 1862. When only eighteen she unwisely married the dissolute James Wallace, and when her father died in 1889 her mother used such money as he had bequeathed to rescue Lucy by paying for a divorce. This left the family with little money in the bank so they had to find a way to support themselves. Dressmaking was one of the few businesses which a woman could start from scratch, for she could begin within her own home. Mrs Kennedy gave her daughter the whole of the ground floor of their home in Davies Street and thus another dressmaker's was founded, to compete against all the other hundreds of dressmakers in town. At this date in the 1890s, it was still normal for middle and upper-class women to have their clothes made for them, rather than buying the poor-quality ready-to-wear.

One of Lucy Kennedy's first successes was making a tea gown for a lady who was going to a house party. A few days later other ladies who had been staying at that house party called to ask for copies of that tea gown. Thus the business grew by small degrees, and after six months it employed four girls. Lucy was lucky in having as a sister the rising novelist Elinor Glyn, who ordered all her clothes from her and as her fame increased she became a leading exhibitor of the creations of Mme Lucy. On the strength of this success, Lucy moved to larger premises in Old Burlington Street and took the trade name of Lucile Ltd. In 1896 a customer going to the Russian coronation took a wardrobe of Lucile day and evening wear, and this resulted in some Russian ladies looking to London and Lucile for their clothes instead of exclusively to Paris.

Lucile's real triumph came in the early 1900s. She married Sir Cosmo Duff Gordon which gave her house a certain prestige, for the dressmaker was now Lady Duff Gordon and this led to higher-class custom. Lucile was very fond of creating romantic clothes, and consequently was commissioned to design dresses for the stage. In 1907 she was invited to design the wardrobe for Lily Elsie in the London production of Franz Lehar's new hit, *The Merry Widow*. Amongst her creations for this operetta was a very large hat which so pleased the public that requests poured in for copies. Enormous hats were the height of fashion, and this particular hat expressed the vogue so well that orders also came from abroad. Hundreds of versions

112 Lily Elsie in Lucile's
Merry Widow costume and
hat, 1907.

were sold throughout Europe and the United States, and Lucile became an international name. Many British ladies switched their orders for clothes from Paris to Lucile, and by 1909 she was making £40,000 a year.

Lucile seized the opportunity of foreign expansion, and in 1909–10 went to New York. She thought the clothes in society there to be poor copies of Parisian couture, and saw this as a good opening for herself. She founded her New York branch with a lot of publicity, making the most of the

American fondess for British titles. Once this was going well she sailed back to England, although not without a traumatic experience, for the ship, the *Titanic*, sank and Lucile and her husband were among the few persons rescued.

In 1911 she opened her Paris branch in the rue Penthièvres, daring to challenge French couture on its own doorstep. The French press made a lot of chauvinist remarks about the folly of a British dressmaker trying to teach the French their own art, which was very shortsighted comment considering that Worth, Redfern and Creed were all flourishing in Paris anyway. What turned mockery into admiration was Lucile's mannequins. She always selected very tall girls, six feet in height, and with striking looks. Two in particular, Dolores and Hebe, became the toasts of London, Paris and New York, and were the first models from a couture house to become famous in their own right since Marie Worth. Faced with these superbly elegant creatures, French criticism withered away.

Romance was the basis of all Lucile's creations. She believed that every gown should be personal, designed to express the individual woman. She favoured soft fabrics such as diaphanous clouds of chiffon, and produced gowns of dreamy allure. Her colour sense was very subtle, blending faded tones until they appeared to melt into each other. She exploited the oriental vogue so beloved of Poiret, designing turbans and trailing gowns in lamés and tulle. The romance was further underlined by giving each dress a lovesick name, such as 'Do you love me?' and 'The sighing sound of lips unsatisfied', yielding the same passionate *frissons* as her sister's novels. She also made underwear romantic, as diaphanous as the gown above it.

113 *Left* Lucile's top model Dolores, silver print by Baron Gayne de Meyer, September 1918.

114 *Centre* Lucile's design for a black silk evening dress, covered with a tunic of black beaded net with beaded fringes, c.1910.

115 *Right* Lucile's design for an evening dress in draped chiffon surmounted by a patterned semi-transparent tunic, and trimmed with ostrich feathers, c.1910.

Hitherto ladies' underwear had been in white linen, for coloured under-clothes were regarded as fast and improper, although scarlet petticoats had been worn under crinolines forty years before. Lucile did not invent coloured underwear, but she promoted it and made it more respectable.

Lucile claimed to have started the first fashion model parades at her 23 Hanover Square headquarters. Paris fashion houses had been presenting their collections on live models for generations, but Lucile's claim may well be true of London. Her first London show was attended by Princess Alice, the Duchess of Westminster and Margot Asquith, who were thus treating London as an important fashion centre. Margot Asquith in particular used to feel that English clothes were hateful, and had gone so far as to invite Poiret to present his collection at 10 Downing Street. This had caused a lot of criticism, for it was the heyday of the British Empire, and national feeling was so strong that even ministers' wives were expected to buy British. Thus Mrs Asquith had to abandon Paris for London, for the sake of Mr Asquith's political reputation, and no doubt other English women followed her example, to Lucile's benefit. A feature of Lucile's fashion parades was the abolition of the black satin *maillot*. This was a garment worn by models which covered their neck, shoulders and arms so that no skin was visible during the daytime, when couture clothes were being shown. Of course it had the added advantage of keeping the clothes free from bodily contact, and therefore clean.[1]

During the First World War, Lucile did much charity work in New York, presenting Dolores and Hebe in clouds of drapery in aid of French war orphans and similar causes. While there she also designed for the *Ziegfield Follies*. Such romantic theatrical wear was the epitome of her style, but once the war was over, it was less and less in vogue. Her fate was not unlike Poiret's in that her exotic taste was rapidly going out of date. Lucile did not attempt to rebuild her Paris branch, and her London house went into a slow decline. She gave dress advice to the wives of *nouveaux riches* for 20 guineas a time, and started writing for the fashion papers. Her circumstances were so reduced that she was more than grateful when her former designer, Molyneux, sent her one of his dresses. She had to sell some of her jewels, and later Molyneux remarked that Lucile had been silly in her choice of jewellery, buying pearls the size of pigeons' eggs which were impossible to sell when she needed the money.[2] She died in 1935.

A rival couture house opened in London in 1906 which was to obtain more important orders than Lucile. This was Reville and Rossiter, founded by two buyers from the department store of Jay's, with premises at 15 and 17 Hanover Square. William Reville Terry was the house designer, and Miss Rossiter the administrator. By 1910 Reville and Rossiter could term themselves court dressmakers, for they were appointed couturiers to the new Queen Mary. By far their most important commission was to design the queen's coronation dress in 1911, of cream satin embroidered in gold threads with a pattern of the English rose, the Scottish thistle and the Irish shamrock, while the hem was decorated with waves representing the seas which bound the British Empire together, surmounted by the tendrils of the lotus of India.

Reville and Rossiter remained the queen's dressmakers throughout the First World War, although economy measures were introduced. Court presentations were abolished between 1914 and 1920, and when they were restarted the Lord Chamberlain introduced new regulations. Whereas Edwardian court trains had been long lengths of brocade lined with silk or satin, padded to give them weight and ornamented with artificial flowers or lace, the post-war court trains had to be no more than 18 inches on the ground, and became much simpler as tastes changed.[3] Such changes robbed the court dressmaker to some extent, for one could not charge so much for simplified gowns as for elaborate ones.

In the early 1920s Reville and Rossiter were still doing well, dressing the queen as the social circuit got under way again. In 1922 they dressed Princess Mary, the Princess Royal, on her marriage to Viscount Lascelles. That same year, when Edwina Ashley became engaged to Lord Mountbatten, she chose Reville for her trousseau (which is the only time the earl remembered accompanying her to a couture house). By then the firm had expanded, with additional premises at 297–9 Oxford Street.

Nevertheless decline was coming their way. In 1923 Norman Hartnell noticed that the actress, Gladys Cooper, was switching her custom from Reville and Rossiter to Molyneux in Paris. By 1927 Lady Mountbatten had changed to Worth. It is not difficult to see why. Reville and Rossiter had learned their ideas about dress in the Edwardian era when clothes were sumptuous, but they were now faced by a vogue for increasingly simpler clothes. They might satisfy their older customers with conservative creations, but the bright young things were not interested in anything so

116 *Left* Lucile, Lady Lucy Duff-Gordon in 1922.

117 *Right* Reville and Rossiter's dress for Queen Mary at the coronation of King George V in 1911. Her purple velvet robe was embroidered by Princess Louise's Ladies Work Society and made up by Messrs Wilkinson and Sons.

PRINCESS MARY'S TROUSSEAU: THE GOING-AWAY DRESS AND OTHERS.

SPECIALLY DRAWN FOR "THE ILLUSTRATED LONDON NEWS" BY OLIVE HEWERDINE.

A simple little dress of grey jersey adorned with pleats and faggot stitching. Worn with a a black satin Breton sailor hat with a ribbon brim.

An exquisite ermine wrap, the ends of which are turned back to form sleeves, and a swathed toque of gold tissue.

An evening dress of wild-rose-pink georgette, embroidered with crystal beads, and finished at the waist with bead roses.

A delicate blue georgette jumper embroidered with white beads, to be worn with the coat and skirt shown opposite

The Going Away Dress. of powder blue charmeuse, embroidered with coral beads, and worn with a black satin hat adorned with a wreath of blue and pink flowers.

A low-waisted coat and skirt of French blue velvet, worn with a black satin hat trimmed with jade green daisies.

CHOSEN BY THE ROYAL BRIDE-TO-BE: BEAUTIFUL DRESSES WHICH COMBINE ELEGANCE AND SIMPLICITY.

118 Reville and Rossiter's trousseau for Princess Mary, in the pastel shades which she loved. Drawing by Olive Hewerdine, February 1922.

119 *Opposite* Norman Hartnell design for a pearl grey chiffon evening dress with ruched points forming a fantail, matching cape, 1933.

stuffy as a court dressmaker. They preferred the youthful styles flooding in from Paris. Thus the firm slowly went downhill, to merge in the mid-1930s with Busvine.

The 1920s saw the foundation of a new English house which was to take over much of Reville's trade. Norman Hartnell started designing clothes when still a youth, and when he went to Cambridge in 1921 he became very active in the dramatic society, creating the theatrical wardrobe. His father

disapproved and said that the drop in his investments meant that he could not finance his son at college, so Hartnell decided to try to become a professional designer. The *Evening Standard* had given a good review of his clothes in a Cambridge production so he asked the journalist concerned for help. She found him a job as designer to the dressmaker, Mme Désiré, in autumn 1922 for £3 a week. While there he was called upon to design clothes for a Buchanan production which involved the actual making of the garments, something Hartnell had to learn desperately as he went along. This brought no fame or fortune, and his job ended at Christmas. He showed some of his designs to Lucile, who published them without paying him, so he had to resort to law to get his due.

With job-hunting proving hopeless, Hartnell decided to take the daring step of opening his own couture house. He had a capital of £300. The news got about the fashion world in London, and an ex-member of Molyneux's staff, Miss Doherty, appointed herself as Hartnell's aid. She found a French *première main* for him, and Hartnell relied very heavily on their expertise, for he could design but had very little knowledge of cut and construction. The year of 1927 saw Hartnell making the pages of English *Vogue* with a taffeta picture frock, and he took the bold step of presenting a collection of his clothes in Paris. This attracted a lot of orders from American buyers, and it was noticed that Hartnell was doing longer skirts before Paris.

The economic slump saw Britain introducing taxes and controls on imports in 1932, which was a help to the growth of British couture. Hartnell's future was assured during this decade when he won British royal custom. Queen Mary ordered three dresses to begin with. In 1935 he made the Duchess of Gloucester's wedding dress and those for the bridesmaids, Princess Elizabeth and Princess Margaret. In 1937 he was called upon to dress the maids of honour at the coronation of King George VI. The following year the new Queen Elizabeth ordered her wardrobe from him for a state visit to France, so Hartnell had to pit his talent against the whole of French couture. The queen preferred a personal style of dressing rather than absolute imitation of fashion, and the king liked the crinolines in the paintings of Winterhalter, so Hartnell was asked to design something similar. As his first dress to appear in *Vogue* had been a picture frock, this was no problem. Lanvin of course had kept the full-skirted style alive; in spring 1937 Schiaparelli showed her waltz dresses and in autumn 1937 Hartnell presented romantic full skirts in satin and tulle. By spring 1938 all Paris had followed suit. The queen's adoption of crinolines for evening was much in keeping with the current trend towards Victorian styles in fashion.

After the war Hartnell's royal commissions multiplied even further. He made the wedding dress for Princess Elizabeth in 1947 and the wardrobes for all the foreign tours she undertook in 1948. His supreme year was in 1953 when he was called upon to design the clothes for the new queen's coronation, for all her ladies, and for many peeresses. In particular he had to design a new type of robe for peeresses with newer titles, following consultation with the Earl Marshall, and this was to be the traditional crimson velvet now topped with a cape of white fur and without sleeves.[4] He died on 8 June 1979 at seventy-seven.

120 Queen Elizabeth opening the Foundling Site Playground in July 1936.

121 As good as anything the French could offer, Norman Hartnell's slinky black satin dinner dress, with cape and fantail skirt of black spangled tulle, December 1934.

122 *Left* Norman Hartnell's design for a dress and jacket in black and white check wool, trimmed with black grosgrain ribbon. Cape-effect sleeves, 1935.

123 *Right* Norman Hartnell's evening dress in black smocking-designed lace, ending in a wide frill of black silk tulle, 1949.

An important development in London in 1937 was the establishment of the International Wool Publicity and Research Secretariat. At the Dominion Wool Conference in Melbourne in January 1937 the growers of wool had voted to set up an organization to protect their common interests, with the headquarters in London. This was a far-sighted move, for rayon was just beginning to steal some of its trade and wool had to adjust to the competition to come from more man-made materials.

Wool is grown mainly in the southern hemisphere, in Australia, New Zealand, South Africa and Uruguay, and processed into textiles principally in the northern industrial hemisphere. From the very first the Secretariat financed research into improving the attraction of wool by such treatments as wrinkle-resistance, permanent creases, colour-fastness, washability and dirt-resistance. It is the duty of the Secretariat to promote the use of wool, to safeguard the producers by introducing price floors, to advise weavers on developments in woollen textiles, to demonstrate how wool must adapt to changes in fashionable taste (as for example from heavy-weight materials to light-weights) and to notify manufacturers of future colour trends. Thus its fabric library tells weavers what wools to make in the year ahead, after analysing current tendencies.[5] From the 1930s French couture was to make increasing use of British woollens, following the great developments in new forms of woollen textiles taking place in this country. Chanel and Schiaparelli were particularly fond of British tweeds.

During the Second World War a similar foundation was established for cotton with the Cotton Board. It upgraded cotton by inviting leading British artists to design for it and by encouraging British couturiers to use it in their collections. Silk has also been protected by the establishment of a similar body so that it can compete against the ever-increasing innovations in artificial fabrics.

The roots of several British couture houses were laid down in the 1930s, although some did not open their businesses until the 1940s. Foremost among these is Hardy Amies. Born in London in 1909, his mother had been both a seamstress at the court dressmaker Mme Durrant and a *vendeuse*, so the boy was aware of clothes from an early age. His first ambition was to be a journalist, however, and his parents were advised to send him to the continent to improve his languages. Accordingly he worked in France as an English tutor and then as assistant to the manager of a German company. He stayed on in Germany working for an English weighing machine company. This was far removed from dressmaking, but it gave him invaluable business experience and a knowledge of personnel management, which were to prove great assets when it came to running his own house. With the rise of Nazism in Germany, Amies was brought back to the United Kingdom and appointed a travelling sales representative.

Hardy Amies' entry into couture was very sudden and unplanned. Late in 1933 he attended a charity dance in the company of his mother's former employers. Afterwards he wrote a description of his companion's dress in a letter which was so vivid that the letter was shown to the company, just at the moment when it was looking for a new designer. It had founded a small couture sportswear firm called Lachasse at the end of the 1920s, with the young Irishman Digby Morton as designer. By the end of 1933 he wished to leave to start his own business, so in 1934 Hardy Amies was brought in as his replacement. Of course the new designer had not worked in this area before, so he had to learn as he went along. He studied those suits already under construction, examined the existing policy on styling and investigated the planning system. By 1935 he had learned so well that he was appointed manager and designer at Lachasse at the age of twenty-six. His principal innovation there was to lengthen jackets for a better fit at the arm and for a neater line. The coronation year brought many American buyers to London in 1937, who found their way to Lachasse, where suits were cheaper than at the main couture houses, and thus many of Hardy Amies' designs were bought for copying in the United States.

With the outbreak of war in 1939 the Lachasse premises behind Berkeley Square were turned into a fire-station. Seeing a call from the Army for linguists, Hardy Amies offered his services and soon found himself in the Intelligence Corps, although he did manage to design a spring collection. Being the designer of a house with another name can be frustrating because all the brilliance of the creations reflects on the house rather than on the designer himself. Not surprisingly therefore Hardy Amies wanted to found his own house. The war made this impossible for the time being, but he did manage to take some steps in that direction. In 1940 Madge Garland, then fashion director at Bourne and Hollingsworth, made it possible for him to have some designs made up in the store's workrooms on condition that the store could also make copies. Worth of London also allowed him to sell designs for evening wear on its own premises.

The German occupation of France meant that Paris was now cut off as a fashion centre, and both the British and American governments sought to take advantage of the situation by encouraging their couturiers to gain dominance in the field. The British government persuaded all the leading London designers to create a joint collection in 1941, which was sent out to South America with a display of luxurious clothes which were now strictly for export only and not available at home in England. Hardy Amies was given leave from the Army to design part of this collection.

This experiment was so successful that it was decided to found a permanent organization in order to give British couture a common voice in dealing with new problems and wartime restrictions. Norman Hartnell was active in bringing the relevant people together, and in 1942 the Incorporated Society of London Fashion Designers was established. Molyneux and Charles Creed had both escaped from France, so they were brought into the group. Molyneux, the *grand doyen* of British couturiers, was appointed chairman, and the other members were Hardy Amies, Creed, Elspeth Champcommunal at Worth, Angèle Delanghe, Norman Hartnell, Digby Morton, Bianca Mosca and Victor Stiebel both at Jacqmar, and Peter Russell. Most of these had their own houses and were presenting collections. In spring 1941 Peter Russell had used cotton most elegantly, Molyneux showed buttons like cigarette ends and pieces of lipstick, Digby Morton was using Viyella, and Hartnell check trimmings. Such variety, however, could not continue under wartime conditions.

In 1942 the Board of Trade introduced the 'Civilian Clothing Order' which restricted the amount of material that could be used in garments, banned unnecessary trimmings and ornaments and limited the number of models that could be introduced. Clothing had already been rationed in June 1941, and to show how to manage under the new limitations the government promoted the 'Utility scheme'. It called upon couturiers to design models to show that clothes could still be attractive and fashionable despite the restrictions, which could then be put into mass production. Molyneux, Hardy Amies, Digby Morton, Bianca Mosca, Peter Russell and Worth all collaborated to create coats, suits, dresses and overalls. Molyneux remarked that austerity might mean the end of frills, but it gave the opportunity to design very well, for the simple dress is often the apex of elegance. Hardy Amies showed how considerable ingenuity could be used to produce an interesting garment from a limited amount of material, by using checks in a counterpoint of straight and bias arrangement. This was far removed from his war-work as head of espionage in Belgium, but ingenuity was a common requirement to both trades!

When the war was over the London couture houses agreed to present their first peacetime collections jointly within the space of one week, for the greater convenience of both buyers and the press. As the clothes were aimed at the export market, austerity restrictions did not apply, and the Board of Trade helped with larger quotas of cloth. As this was the first big fashion barrage in Britain for six years it attracted buyers from the United States,

126 *Left* The trend towards a more feminine line. Hardy Amies topcoat in black velour 'Eminence', with more rounded shoulders, and padded hips, the curves emphasized by curved pockets. Black felt hat with a cluster of multicoloured feathers by Mme Simone Mirman, winter 1946.

the Dominions, Europe and the Middle East. The most common trend exhibited for spring 1946 was towards a more feminine line, with rounded shoulders and greater use of colour.[6]

When Lieutenant-Colonel Hardy Amies was demobbed in 1945 he could at last found his own house. He acquired a bomb-damaged mansion at 14 Savile Row, once the home of the dramatist Sheridan, and opened as an independent couturier on 1 January 1946. Given all the work he had done at Lachasse and during the war, his name was already well known both here and abroad, and he had received orders from stores in Chicago and California before he presented his first collection in Savile Row. His declared aim was to make suits more curvaceous. From his acquaintance with Molyneux he knew that whilst extraordinary creations might interest the press, they were not the sort of clothes women wanted to buy. He therefore limited the number of funny or dramatic models in any one collection in favour of a greater number of obviously wearable clothes. This struck the right note, and Amies was patronized by such an elegant star as

127 *Opposite right*
Hardy Amies suit 'Easter Sunday' in the new navy with a faintly green tinge. It has raglan shoulders, the line of which is repeated in the curved edge of the jacket held by three silver buttons. The basque of the jacket is flaired out, and the top of the skirt is seamed and pocketed to give roundness. The correct length for straight skirts with the New Look is 13 inches (33 cms) from the ground, March 1949.

128 Hardy Amies topcoat 'Horizon' in gun-metal and pale blue tweed with frame collar, the skirt cut in an interplay of straight and bias material. Tweed from Linton Tweeds Ltd. Such coats were much sought after by his American customers, March 1949.

129 Hardy Amies ball gown 'Foam' in Nottingham lace edged with volants of tulle, and with three tulle underskirts. A single layer of lace covers the shoulders without hiding them. A dress of timeless romance, March 1949.

Vivien Leigh. Princess Elizabeth was attracted by his designs, and after she became queen Amies was created 'by appointment Dressmaker to Her Majesty'.

Ever the astute businessman, Amies went to the United States in 1946 where he obtained £8,000's worth of orders, and subsequently he made such trips a regular feature of his management. By the 1950s Amies had a staff of one hundred and forty-five working on the cutting and sewing of garments, with another forty-eight engaged in design, management, sales and despatch. He opened one of the first ready-to-wear boutiques in London, with a staff of twenty-one. Such numbers were modest in comparison with the size of some Paris houses. Nevertheless Hardy Amies has built up one of the most successful British couture houses, with an ever-widening diversity of interests into menswear, knitwear, hosiery, sportswear, travel goods and household materials, resulting eventually in annual sales worth 160 million dollars. This is a house which looks set to continue for a good many years to come.[7]

British couture houses were fairly numerous at the time and were to do quite well after the war. Charles Creed of the famous tailoring family set up his English house in 1946. Educated at Stowe between 1923 and 1928, he was then sent by his father to Vienna to study tailoring and art, and later to Linton Tweeds, Carlisle, to learn about weaving. Creed next went to New York where he worked for the department store of Bergdorf Goodman, after which he began designing for American wholesale firms, first for Beller and then for the big manufacturer, Philip Magnone. Only after this wide education did Creed's father agree to take his son into the family firm in Paris to design ladies' couture wear, and by the late 1930s he was visiting Hollywood to dress filmstars. With the outbreak of war Creed had to leave France, and he returned to England to join the Army. Like Amies he sometimes managed to do some designing when on leave, working for Fortnum and Mason on these occasions. Once the war was over he went to New York and won a contract to design clothes for Magnone again, but this time the garments were to carry his own label. Following this he opened his London house and helped it to flourish by repeating what he had done before the war, namely, taking small collections over to the United States which were specially designed for that market. Very much a ladies' man, Creed became renowned for his superbly tailored suits, thereby maintaining the family reputation in that field. When he died in 1966 it was just as couture was going into a serious decline.

Angèle Delanghe came to London from Antwerp in 1915. At first she worked for Eva Lutyens, the dressmaker, then started her own house. Like other women designers she often created her clothes on an old dummy rather than drawing the idea first. Whilst she was important enough to be asked to join the Incorporated Society of London Fashion Designers in 1942, she was not the sort of creator who regularly made headlines in *Vogue*. Her forte was the little black dress which women could rely on, rather than sensation. She said the one bane of her existence was having an English husband who had no interest in clothes whatsoever.

Digby Morton came to London from Ireland. His first ambition had been to be an architect, but as the training took much longer than he could afford, he turned his attention to dress design. In 1928 he became the first designer at Lachasse, leaving in 1934 to found his own establishment. Regularly featured in *Vogue* from then on and throughout the 1940s and 1950s, Morton showed his expertise in taking soft Irish tweed and sculpting it into immaculately clean-lined suits. With an eye on the American market he too took collections over the Atlantic, although when he set out in 1940 he was torpedoed and was rescued after twenty hours in an open boat. Another trip in 1946 was more peaceful and much more profitable. Like Creed he was involved with non-couture productions before other houses were, opening a ready-to-wear department as early as 1939.

130 *Opposite* Charles Creed
suit in red ottoman with long
sleeved brocade waistcoat
maintaining the family's
tradition of excellent
tailoring. Black straw hat by
Suzy, February 1938.

Another of the original members of the Incorporated Society was Bianca
Mosca. She had spent fifteen years working as a designer for Schiaparelli,
before coming to London. During the war she worked for Jacqmar, and in
1946 she went on to open her own business. Unlike native British designers
she did not care much for sharply tailored suits, and concentrated her talents
on soft clothes and good teagowns.

Victor Stiebel came from South Africa. Like Hartnell he went to
Cambridge, but failed his finals, his heart really being set on designing
clothes. He went to Reville and Rossiter and served a three-year
apprenticeship in dressmaking and cutting, starting as the proverbial
picker-up of pins. He was thus one of the few couturiers in London who did
come up from the very bottom of a couture house. In 1932 he opened his

131 Angèle Delanghe:
evening dress with bodice
and basque in milky blue
moiré and the skirt of black
corded silk. Drawing by
Louise Ambler, November
1946.

192

own salon in Bruton Street, when *Vogue* first gave him a mention. He loved creating romantic clothes such as flowing evening dresses and summery Ascot gowns. This made him much in demand for the stage in the 1930s, when he dressed many a production. Vivien Leigh looked at her best in his full-skirted gowns of tulle or velvet and silk. During the war Stiebel went to Jacqmar and remained there afterwards. He said that for him design was a cerebral affair, a gown appearing in his mind in all its detail before he set it down on paper, or else leaping into his thoughts when he gazed at a particularly fine piece of fabric. This was the masculine approach to design as opposed to that shown by most women designers. The Army commandeered Stiebel for camouflage during the war, but this did not affect his style, which remained as romantic in the 1950s as it had been in the 1930s.

Elspeth Champcommunal began by studying painting in Florence and Paris, which gave her a highly developed colour sense when it came to opening her own salon in Paris. The economic slump forced her to close and Worth's sent her to London in 1936 to design for their British branch. She hated regimentation and avoided the military look of some tailored wear in favour of clothes that were both feminine and romantic, conjuring beautiful

132 *Opposite* Vivien Leigh in Victor Steibel's evening gown of magenta taffeta bordered with turquoise, typical of the romantic clothes he loved to make, 1937.

133 *Above* Victor Steibel studying a roll of fabric draped on a model, thinking up ideas rather than playing around with the material, January 1935.

creations out of lace.[8] Some of her earlier designs were featured in *Vogue* in 1928, and she had been editor of the British edition when it first started. Perhaps her most important customer in London, after Princess Alice, was Lady Louis Mountbatten. From a bright young thing of the 1920s the countess had matured into a woman much involved in war work and charities. This meant that her need for couture clothes diminished, but when she needed anything special she went to Worth in London, most notably just after the war when she and her husband went out to India as the last British vicereine and viceroy. As a British vicereine had been dressed by the great Worth in 1877, it was highly appropriate that the last vicereine should also be dressed by Worth, albeit by the London branch.

The Incorporated Society was never a rigid organization, for its membership was fluid. Mention should be made of John Cavanagh, who had been Molyneux's secretary in Paris in the 1930s and thus had a good knowledge of the running and design sides of a couture house, although he did not open his own London house until 1952. Other members were Mattli, Michael at Lachasse, Michael Sherard, Ronald Paterson, Rhavis and Clive. The membership varied as some left to retire, others to concentrate on ready-to-wear manufacture or on running boutiques. Nevertheless, the Incorporated Society was to remain a considerable force throughout the 1950s and into the 1960s, promoting British fashion around the world and particularly in the United States.

The decline of London couture was parallel to the decline in Paris, and not a peculiarly English problem. As young customers insisted more and more on 'doing their own thing', and even the daughters of duchesses were happy to run around in jeans all day long, interest in haute couture fashion diminished. There was not sufficient demand to keep a score of couture houses in business, and the number rapidly contracted in the 1960s, the great survivors being Hartnell, Amies and Lachasse. Haute couture, says Hardy Amies, is a profitable extravagance, and there will always be just enough rich clients to keep a few couture houses open. Nevertheless, even the survivors have had to diversify their interests, Hartnell designing for Berketex and subsequently consultant to Great Universal Stores, while Amies has connexions with Carrington, Viyella, Debenham's, Hepworth's and Vantona Textiles, as well as with numerous companies in Australia, Canada, New Zealand, Japan and the United States. The surviving Parisian houses have undertaken similar links with industry and trade, for that is the best guarantee of their continued existence.

One growing problem, however, even for the survivors, is the decline in available staff. Haute couture depends upon the patient labour of women sewing with their hands, but such employees can now find better paid work in factories making mass-produced clothing. Art colleges can turn out dozens of students who would like to be fashion or textile designers, but precious few who are willing to restrict themselves to sewing. As in other creative industries, it is the shortage of craftsmen which is becoming increasingly critical, and even a total craft revival would be unlikely to persuade many women to devote their lives to stitching away in a couture workroom.

11 Paris 1939–1950: the War and After

When the German troops were marching on Paris, Elsa Schiaparelli asked Lucien Lelong, as head of the Chambre Syndicale de la Haute Couture, what Parisian couturiers ought to do. Lelong turned to Molyneux, who offered to convert his branch in Biarritz into three parts so that they could all work there together. Machinery was sent ahead and Molyneux, Lelong and Schiaparelli hurried to Bordeaux just as the Germans were entering Paris. A meeting of couturiers was called there, and Balenciaga, Heim, Patou and Piguet were all represented in addition to the other three. They agreed to wait and see what would develop, but then the French government capitulated to the enemy. Britain, however, and Germany were still at war, and it was suddenly very dangerous for people with British passports to be caught in France. All plans for a couture establishment in Biarritz were dropped, and Charles Creed and Captain Edward Molyneux travelled to England on the last ship to get away from Bordeaux. Spring 1940 was the last time the outside world heard the fashion news from Paris until the Liberation of 1944.

Schiaparelli had a contract to go and lecture in the United States so she went there, but Lelong felt that as he was the official head of the haute couture industry it was his duty to return to occupied Paris and try to defend the system as best he could. He had not been back in the capital long before the Germans broke into the offices of the Chambre Syndicale and seized all the documents relating to exports. Lelong was informed that the French couture industry was to be moved to Berlin and Vienna, to merge with German dress manufacture in order to create a major new export industry for the Reich.[1] Lelong knew that this would be the death of French couture. He went to Berlin and argued that couture could not survive if it were split up and moved abroad. It was not simply a case of transporting the staff of couture houses together with their machinery, for that was not the whole of the couture world. Beneath it and uniquely numerous in Paris, were all the little manufacturers of the hundred and one accessories, decorations and trimmings. It was simply not possible to transport all of them as well, or divide them all between Vienna and Berlin. Haute couture and its suppliers had to stay together. At last the Germans relented, and in 1941 Lelong decided to reopen his own Paris salon and set about recruiting staff.

One of the first persons Lelong turned to was the young designer, Pierre Balmain. Born in May 1914 at St Jean-de-Maurienne near Aix-les-Bains in Savoy, Balmain's background was a family dress shop run by his aunts in which his mother, as the youngest, worked as the salesgirl. She married the head of the local drapery business, so it is hardly surprising that her son should develop an interest in clothes and textiles. Mme Balmain, however, did not think that dress designing would be a very secure profession for her son, and encouraged him to think of something more reliable. Thus when Balmain went to study in Paris he chose architecture, but he continued to draw dresses in his own time. A common interest in architecture and dress design was by no means unparalleled. Apart from Balmain's contemporary, Digby Morton, who also wanted to be an architect, there had been architects who had also been costume designers, such as Inigo Jones and Godwin. Perhaps the common thread was an interest in structure and proportion.

Balmain managed to sell some of his dress designs to Piguet, and encouraged by this he next went to Molyneux in 1934. Molyneux did not care for Balmain's drawings but told him to call again the following week. When Balmain returned the reaction was still not favourable, but Molyneux said he would give the young man a try. Balmain was to continue with his architectural studies in the morning, but afternoons he could spend at Molyneux's for one month, with a salary of 500 francs. Inevitably he made some mistakes, for he had no idea how to turn a drawing into a *toile*, but at the end of the month Molyneux engaged him on a full-time basis and the architectural studies ceased.

In 1936 Balmain was called up to do his military service, but he contrived to be stationed in Paris where he managed to continue some work at Molyneux's. This period in that great couture house was of immense importance to the young designer. Balmain was deeply impressed by Molyneux's belief in simplicity, by his horror of gaudy detail and by his fondness for beige. When he decided to leave the house in 1939 it was because he felt that he was not being given any serious responsibility. Balmain next went to Lelong's, but when the German invasion came he went back home to Savoy, to be with his mother in Aix-les-Bains. The town was quite crowded with wealthy refugees from Paris who, on hearing that a Parisian couturier had come to the area, started to order some clothes. Balmain thus set up a little couture business of his own, and was running this when Lelong phoned him in 1941 to ask him to come back and help rebuild Parisian couture. Balmain obeyed and found himself placed in a studio to work alongside another new designer, older than himself, Christian Dior.[2]

Born in Normandy in 1905, Dior was the son of a wealthy manufacturer of chemical fertilizer. He too considered architecture as a career but his parents were not enthusiastic and he was sent to study for the *corps diplomatique* at the Ecole des Sciences Politiques. By 1928 Dior had turned his attention to founding a small art gallery, which went quite well, but in 1931 his father lost all his money through investing in real estate, and all the family's possessions including Christian's art gallery had to be sold off to pay the father's debts. Young Dior had made several friends in the art and design world and it was they who now came to his aid. One in particular, Jean Ozenne, the fashion designer, taught him to sketch and sold some of his designs. Dior therefore concentrated on working as a freelance designer. In 1937 Piguet bought some of his drawings, and in 1938 he engaged Dior as a house designer.

At the outbreak of war Dior was called up, but when France fell he went south to be with his father and sister, who were now farming a smallholding. Piguet invited Dior to return as designer, but he dallied so long in the sun that by the time Dior did return to Paris Piguet had engaged someone else, Castillo. Once again friends came to Dior's salvation and introduced him to Lelong, who took him on to share designing duties with Balmain.[3] Lelong had hopes of founding a school for couture designers, and appointing two trained designers to his staff can be seen as a step in this direction.

During the German occupation, natural fabrics like wool and silk became extremely rare. The French population had to make do with artificial materials, which were rationed under a points system, but Lelong managed to get a special allowance of points for the couture trade, based on pre-war and not current business. He also obtained permission for couture creations to escape clothes rationing, in order to keep the industry alive. The prospect of unrationed clothes in wartime attracted a wider range of clientele than ever before, with the middle rank of society beginning to attend the salons. There were also two new sorts of customer created by the war itself, the wives of German officers and the wives of profiteers from the black market. Dior used to remark that this sort of customer would be shot, come the Liberation.

The Germans restricted both the production of textiles and the number of couture houses, so the collections were of necessity of a much smaller scale than before the war. Whereas up to three thousand model dresses used to be shown per season, now the number was down to about a hundred. Some items like ribbon were not rationed, so haute couture designers used lots of it. Indeed ingenuity was now the key to creation, and hats were made of scraps such as rags, newspapers and wood shavings. Twenty houses managed to remain open, doing all they could to keep their staffs together for fear of their being sent to labour camps in Germany. As much as possible they cheated the German authorities over their points allowance, and schemed to help each other if any one house should fall foul of the administration. Thus when the Germans ordered Balenciaga and Mme Grès to close for two weeks on the eve of their collections for exceeding the permitted amount of material in their clothes, the other couture houses quietly finished their models for them.

To the Allied Nations outside, locked in the war against Germany, this continuation of couture with German customers stank of collaboration with the enemy. For Lelong and the couturiers he was trying to protect, however, the viewpoint was very different. They were living under enemy occupation. If they had done the highly moral thing, and closed down rather than deal with the Nazis, it would have been suicide. The staff would have been conscripted to do forced labour and the whole structure of the trade would have been broken. It was better to deal with the devil than to kill off the industry altogether, for once the expertise was lost it would take years and years to regain it, come the peace. In their view it was essential to keep something going, no matter how much a shadow of its former self, so that when the Liberation did come, Paris couture could blossom again. Such a far-sighted policy was difficult for the Allies to understand, preoccupied as they were with the immediate struggle.

" *But I'd feel a perfect FOOL!* "

Paris was liberated in August 1944, and the outside world could once more see photographs of French high fashion, but it was astonished at what was revealed. In Britain clothes were rationed and in the United States restrictions had been introduced, but here was unrationed Parisian haute couture showing dresses using quantities of material in huge sleeves and skirts. From both sides of the Atlantic came official condemnation of such wasteful creations, which British and American women did not have the means to copy. There were photographs too of very rich Parisiennes in new fur coats and silk stockings, the sort of things that were unobtainable in England. Of course such women who could afford the prices of the luxury shops around the Place de la Concorde represented only a tiny minority of the Parisian population. The ordinary woman of Paris could not afford stockings, for rayon ones cost 150 francs and silk ones 700 francs. Most people wore wooden-soled shoes and cardigans made of string. There were some pullovers in the luxury shops at 3,000 francs and lace blouses at 2,500 francs, but only for the very privileged few. In fact the French government had to appeal for foreign aid to help clothe the ordinary population, which made the luxury on show in the couture salons appear particularly reprehensible.

The foreign outcry at extravagant styles made its impact. By the autumn of 1945 the Paris fashion houses had sobered down, and the amount of material used in a dress was limited to three metres. After the exaggerated and bulky line that had been flaunted in the face of the Nazis, austerity was producing a simpler elegance. Nevertheless, as British *Vogue* pointed out in January 1946, some Parisian dresses still contravened United Kingdom austerity regulations by the use of buttons for ornamentation and unnecessary wastage of fabric in such details as turn-back cuffs and pocket flaps.

The peace saw the return of such old favourites as Captain Molyneux and Elsa Schiaparelli to Paris, who both showed collections in the autumn of 1945, and the opening of brand-new couture houses. In 1944 as the Germans were retreating from the city, Balmain decided the time had come to go solo and to leave Lelong. He opened with a staff of twenty-four and his first collection was very casual in its organization, but his audience was kindly disposed towards the newcomer and all went well. Cecil Beaton was there and reported Balmain's talent to the British Embassy. By 1946

135 Paris couture dresses, suits and coats which contravened British austerity regulations with the unessential use of buttons, cuffs and pocket flaps, January 1946.

Maggy Rouff's dinner dress, row of buttons as ornamentation only

Lelong's wool dress Double row rouleau at neck. Cuffs turned back

Molyneux suit. Turn-back cuffs and buttoned flap on pockets

Piguet. Wool dress shoulder buttons as ornament, not fastening

Lelong. One too many buttons and used as ornamentation only

BALENCIAGA'S
STRAIGHT NARROW COAT

137 The trend towards the New Look. Balenciaga's straight coat with the shoulder line softer and rounder, and the skirt below the knee. Drawing by Gorau, January/February 1946.

Balmain was being hailed in the fashion press as the new star in couture, and the Duchess of Kent, the Duchess of Windsor and Princess Radziwill were placing orders. Balmain felt that it was a very good time to start, for people were eager for 'new beauties' after the misery of the war.

In those early days Balmain was noted for introducing square necklines set low, and blouses based on workers' tops. A bronze satin evening blouse embroidered in jet showed his flair for beautiful gala wear. In 1947 Balmain was recuperating after an accident when Dior was stealing the fashion headlines, but on his recovery he went off to Australia as the first couturier to visit that country, and then back to France by way of the United States and its department stores, gathering orders as he went. In 1949 he produced his oriental line, and he went on to flourish throughout the 1950s, known as a creator of superb clothes rather than as a revolutionary launcher of new fashions. When he did try one bold innovation, a back-to-the-1920s look, it was a big flop. He was on much surer ground with his luxurious creations.[4]

Christian Dior did not open his own house until 1947, when Boussac had agreed to finance him.[5] Thus Lelong lost both the designers he had looked upon as his successors. Dior's first collection in February 1947 was such a sensation that it has confused the true picture ever since. It became a modern legend that Dior brought back feminity to fashion, but the truth is that this movement was already under way in London, Paris and New York. After the harsh brutality of war and the very square masculine line of wartime clothes, a yearning for more feminine softness in peacetime was universal. There was a trend towards longer skirts; in autumn 1945

" Using all a chap's coupons to get a New Look is bad enough, but making him walk behind because he's so shabby . . . really!"

Balenciaga showed hemlines 15 inches from the ground, while in New York in June 1946 American designers were showing hems three inches below the knee, sometimes in a flared skirt and sometimes in an uneven handkerchief hem. In October 1946 British *Vogue* greeted the latest Parisian collections with the headline 'Paris revels in femininity', for the general line was softening up and becoming more subtly feminine, with figure-hugging clothes. The London collections of March 1946 were noted for the introduction of rounded shoulders after years of square ones. Thus the movement was there already; Dior did not invent it. What he did was to adopt the current trend and take it to its extremity, exaggerating it to incorporate all the elements that were considered truly feminine.

Dior's Corolle line of spring 1947, later to be termed the New Look, was the first completely different fashion since the war. It was not a gentle variation but an all-out replacement of the existing mode. Angles were banished and the emphasis was upon an exaggeration of a woman's natural shape. Bodices were tight, waists were squeezed in and skirts burst out in quantities of material, with hems only one foot from the ground. The general outline was not far removed from the feminine styles that had come into fashion in 1915/16 when Dior was ten.

The New Look was welcomed by women for its complete change of

138 *Left* Luxury in the midst of shortages. Dior's New Look coat and heavily pleated dress requiring material by the metre. Drawing by Eric, 1947.

139 *Right* Acquiring a New Look wardrobe required more clothing coupons than one person was allowed. Cartoon by Lee, 1947.

emphasis. It represented a retreat from women doing the same jobs as men during the war, and was back to the little woman in the kitchen with a vengeance. The new mode was not welcomed, however, in official circles. Dropping the hemline and making skirts much fuller was flying in the face of clothes rationing and restraint. In Britain, Sir Stafford Cripps, President of the Board of Trade, denounced it, as did some women MPs. Typical of some of the criticism was the report by Marjorie Beckett in *Picture Post* for 27 September 1947. With the headline 'Paris Forgets this is 1947', she declared that Dior's fashion was a return to the wealthy indolence of the Edwardian period. Here was a style presented to the world at the very moment when women did not have enough fabrics to copy it, when they could not afford it, when they did not have the leisure to enjoy it, and when there was still weak and hungry women without the strength to even wear such elaborate masses of material: 'We are back in the days when fashion was the prerogative of the leisured wealthy woman, and not the everyday concern of typist, saleswoman or housewife.'

What was shocking after so many years of shortages was the amount of material used in Dior's skirts. One day dress with an 18-inch waist had 50 yards of stuff in the skirt. Others had 20 to 30 yards of flute-pleated tweed. Evening gowns were even fuller. How could a woman with a limited number of clothing coupons afford such creations? Such extravagance could not be copied exactly, but by the end of the year even ready-to-wear manufacturers were adopting an impression of the style, with longer skirts, although using very much less material. The French government assisted the new fashion by mounting presentations at French embassies around the globe. The result was that the British royal family and Eva Peron in Argentina succumbed to the New Look. Officialdom might frown, but women liked it, and Maison Dior was flooded with orders. Extra staff had to be recruited, and extra premises found, as Dior frantically organized an immediate expansion. His backer, Boussac, sent him a business manager, Jacques Rouet, and soon Maison Dior was getting into top gear as the most important couture house of the day.

Dior's success did not prevent other couturiers from doing well, even if they did not hit the headlines so loudly. Jacques Fath continued now taking premises in the avenue Pierre I de Serbie. For some of the leading couturiers their wives have been both their inspiration and their greatest advertisement, and it was now no less so for Fath than it had been for Worth, Poiret and Lelong. Mme Geneviève Fath was dressed impeccably by her husband as the living epitome of his style, and wherever she went women were influenced into placing orders. Business thrived, and soon Fath was employing four hundred workers, which rose to six hundred by the time he died in 1954.

As the 1940s turned into the 1950s, fashion was to see two predominant styles, the full and the narrow. Jacques Fath was a promoter of the narrow skirt, creating pencil-slim dresses which imposed the same sort of problems for mobility as the hobble skirt forty years before. The full look he exploited mostly in huge coats with enormous collars and swinging backs. He had a flair for excitement, not only producing exaggerated clothes but brightening

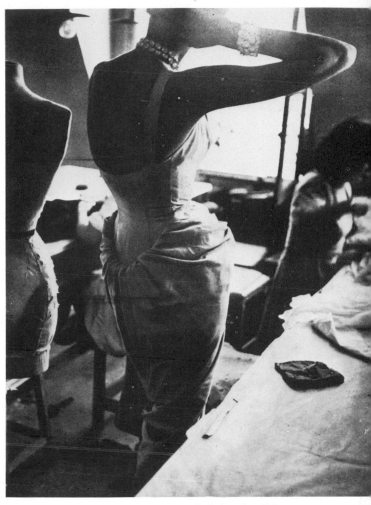

up colours considerably. Whereas a lady had always dressed in subdued tones, Fath used bright yellow, blue and green with abandon. He even introduced pale tones into bridal wear – soft pinks and blues – instead of the inevitable white. Fath was something of a showman in the tradition of Poiret. After his July collections he would throw lavish parties at his château, inviting the press, buyers, private customers and friends. His celebrations always had a theme, such as Hollywood, Versailles or Brazil, so that the guests could dress up in the appropriate costume. Needless to say, such festivities were wonderful publicity and showed Fath occupying a niche which the shy and retiring Dior could not have filled.

In addition to female couture, Fath set new examples in menswear, helping to change the image of the gentleman into a more relaxed and casual creature. He sported a tartan dinner jacket for evenings, and wore a polo-neck sweater at work instead of a formal suit. His ease of manner and dislike of formality were also manifest in his pioneering approach to ready-to-wear, as seen earlier. Fath lived at a frantic pace, for he knew his time was limited, dying at forty-two of leukemia, in 1954.[6]

140 *Left* Another Dior innovation, the strapless dinner dress worn with a big hat. Velvet bodice, and a skirt of faille cut in deep, petal-shaped folds that encircle the body with swinging movement, October 1947.

141 *Right* The alternative to the very full skirt, the narrow line, in Dior's model Zerline in ice blue satin, the bodice highly structured in boned panels, and the drapery of the skirt tucked in. Photographed in one of Dior's workrooms, October 1947.

142 One of the *trompe l'oeil* transmutations in which Jacques Fath delighted, the street-into-cocktail-dress. *Left*, bodice of shimmering black and white lamé, above a buttoned black skirt with flat moiré bow threaded through below the waist. *Right*, the addition of a tight little jacket converts the ensemble into a business suit. The stiff white collar with the rose pinned to it was a feature throughout his collection that year, October 1949.

In complete contrast to the flamboyant Fath were the austere Balenciaga, whom Fath considered far too serious and severe. This illustrates two contrary philosophical approaches co-existing within the same specialized world. There were some couturiers for whom fashion had to be fun and excitement, and there were others for whom dress was a most exacting art demanding the highest standards obtainable from the human hand. For Balenciaga couture clothes had to be nothing less than perfect, in the true tradition of the craft.

As a Spaniard Balenciaga had a feeling for the drama of black, either on its own or in stark contrast with white. These two shades repeatedly recurred in his collections throughout his career. Consequently he had many customers from Spain and South America, and the two couturiers whom Balanciaga himself trained were also Latins. André Courrèges, who joined Balenciaga in 1950, came from Pau in the Basque district. Born in 1923, he had studied civil engineering before turning to fashion and textiles. When Courrèges left to found his own house he found a replacement in Emanuel Ungaro, who was born in Aix-en-Provence of Italian parents in 1933. Thus the atmosphere at Balenciaga's was always very southern and severe in the Spanish manner.

Balenciaga was a hard task master, a very difficult man to please. As he had begun by designing, cutting and making clothes all by himself, he insisted on his trainee designers acquiring the same range of abilities. It was not enough that they could draw well or cut out a pattern; for him they had

to do both, and sew the dress together and fit it. Balenciaga lived for couture and demanded a total commitment to it from his staff. He was a classicist in the tradition of Molyneux and Chanel. Elegance meant the elimination of unnecessary detail, stripping a gown down to its essential parts. He subscribed to the creed that innovations had to be gradual and subtle.

143 Only perfection will do. Balenciaga's dramatic purity shown in a white *fin de journée* suit trimmed with black lace, 1946.

Sudden change was to him vulgar and bad taste. His clothes had to be studied in order to see the modifications for they never screamed their novelty aloud. Accordingly his clothes had the same dateless quality as many a creation by Molyneux, and a model from his house could still look very smart and attractive twenty years after its presentation.

Balenciaga's greatest influence was to be in the 1950s, when the gradual changes in his highly sculptured suits were copied throughout the trade. He was hailed as the leader of fashion, the doyen of the industry, the maintainer of standards who could never descend to a cheap trick or a garish change. Despite such success, however, Balenciaga was to grow more and more disenchanted with the post-war world. He created extremely expensive clothes which used only the best materials and into which many hours of construction had gone to achieve a faultless finish. The market for such creations was declining, and the world no longer wanted perfection for the few.

Balenciaga's true heir was not one of the couturiers he trained himself but Hubert de Givenchy. Born in 1927, Givenchy had studied both art and law before turning to couture. He served a long apprenticeship as an assistant designer, working for Lelong in 1945–6, for Piguet in 1946–8, for Fath in 1948–9, and for Schiaparelli in 1949–51. In 1952 he opened his own house, and his dedication to his craft impressed Balenciaga, who befriended and encouraged the new couturier and saw him as a maintainer of the same standards of dressmaking as himself.[7]

This was the period which was to witness the end of the oldest haute couture house, Worth. Jacques Worth died at Cannes in 1941, and his eldest son Roger, the firm's designer, became head of the house. The second son, Maurice, had worked with his father in administration between 1937 and 1939, but was called up on war service until 1941. In 1943 his brother called him back to the family firm and appointed him *secrétaire général*, a post which he held until 1952.

For the fourth generation of the Worth family to work in haute couture life was full of problems. The number of royal houses which had sustained the salon through the 1920s and 1930s was rapidly shrinking. First the Spanish monarchy collapsed and then the Italian one, depriving Maison Worth of its Bourbon custom. The number of clients who wanted good clothes rather than avant-garde fashions was also declining. The idea that a lady wore excellent rather than sensational clothes was being replaced by a more competitive spirit to keep up with the very latest styles. In the old days American customers would buy their Worth gowns and then put them away for a couple of years before wearing them, for it used to be considered bad taste to be too smart. That attitude no longer applied.

In 1952 Roger Worth decided to retire from designing after twenty-seven years. Maurice Worth now became head of the firm. In 1954 Paquin, that other old house, itself facing difficulties, made a take-over offer, which Maurice accepted. Thus Maison Worth came to an end just four years short of its centenary, although Parfums Worth were continued as a separate entity under Roger Worth. In 1956 Paquin itself found that it could no longer continue, and closed after sixty-five years in the business. Neither house had diversified its interests in the same way as the newer houses were doing.

Compared to *la belle époque* and the 1920s and 1930s, the post-war period produced very little female talent in the couture field. Only Nina Ricci from Italy had founded a successful house on the old model. Girls with designing talent were no longer interested in setting up business in the old pattern, with luxurious salons and extremely expensive clothes. Their ability was to be directed towards the boutique, producing individual designs for the ready-to-wear market. Their original creations were sold straight to the street, and their customers were buying a look that was independent of the dictates of haute couture. From the 1950s the young were less and less concerned with what Paris had to say on the subject of dressing like a lady.

This teenage revolt was mainly an Anglo-American development and not a French one. With the advent of peace many married couples decided that it was now safe to rear families, and the result was a baby boom, which meant that by the late 1950s there were more teenagers than before. All these youngsters had to be clothed, and the British and American ready-to-wear industry was well placed to cope with the demand, being organized for mass-production, and already having retail outlets available in chain stores. France and the rest of the Continent had neither the production nor retail outlets to meet such a youthful market.

Britain had taken the lead in raising the standard of design in ready-to-wear clothing when her couturiers had supervised the Utility scheme during the war. This step was further consolidated when London's Royal College of Art started its fashion design course in 1948, training designers for the mass market, and art colleges around the country also established courses based on the RCA's example. The graduates from these design courses began to emerge in the 1950s, and being young themselves they thought in terms of what their contemporaries needed, and not what Paris said they ought to have. Mary Quant from Goldsmiths College set up her Chelsea shop, Bazaar, in 1956, and disliking the garments sold by the manufacturers, decided to start making her own.[8] John Stephen opened in Carnaby Street in 1959, providing colourful clothes for young men, in place of the grey suits and white shirts of tradition. By the early 1960s London was seen as the centre of young fashion, with Paris being looked upon as an irrelevant dowager. Two graduates from the RCA, Foale and Tuffin, opened the first boutique in a department store, with the '21 Shop' at Wooland's in 1962, Biba opened in 1966 after two years as a mail order firm, 'Miss Selfridge' began in the same year, and Bus Stop started in 1967. Their common aim was to make fashion available to everyone, not in seasonal collections on the French model, but in a constant stream of instant designs.

Initially haute couture was to be very successful in the early 1950s, and its innovations were greeted with intensive coverage by the fashion press, but in a way its success was also its undoing. Practically every season had to have a sweeping change to make the headlines. There was the Y line, and the A line, and the H line, then the sack, all from Dior. Hemlines were modified, an inch off here, two inches on there. Skirts went from wide to narrow, and back to wide again. Such dictates were followed faithfully by the ready-to-wear industry, but any woman devoted to keeping in the fashion found that she might have to change her shape every year to keep up with all the variations. Dior's alphabetical lines were all examples of a male designer imposing an abstract shape upon the female body, instead of starting from the nature of that body itself.

Such a plethora of absurd shapes was all very well for the rich, but were too extreme for housewives and secretaries, and still more so for teenagers. What did such changes have to do with their way of life? In the past Paris could have replied that it did not care what the young thought, for it made clothes for those with money. But from the 1950s more and more youngsters were earning, and their combined purchasing power was far greater in value than the sales of haute couture. This was a development which Paris could not afford to ignore. It was Jacques Fath and Balmain who started designing for the ready-to-wear industry in France and the United States, but it was not until 1964 that Courrèges and Pierre Cardin started to design way-out clothes aimed at the young above all, with their space age fashions.

There was one great enemy of folly in dress still alive, be it the extremes of haute couture or the absurdities of youthful fantasy, and this was Coco Chanel. In 1954 at the age of seventy-one she actually came out of retirement in order to make clothes simple and sensible again. She did exactly as she had done before the war, creating garments which were casual, youthful and easy to wear. Her old tenet of understatement was resurrected. At first reaction was divided. Chanel was accused of not having changed, but by the end of the year her sophisticated simplicity was winning adherents. Here were classic outfits which did not change wildly every season and which devotees could wear for years and years. Chanel was to enjoy an immense success, and by the time of her death in 1971 it had made her a legend, but other couturiers lacked the wisdom to appreciate the eternal value of a single look which only changes by degrees.

Despite her age Chanel was by no means blind to the enormous changes afoot. She declared that instead of making clothes for just a few private customers she was now going to sell dresses by the thousand, showing her awareness of the importance of designing for the popular market, where the money was. One of the buyers who was able to bring Chanel to the masses was Geoffrey Wallis of Wallis shops who wished to make good design available to all. Other Paris houses, such as Nina Ricci, St Laurent, Cardin and Lanvin, were all to start designing for the ready-to-wear mass market; they had to adapt in order to stay in business. Couture houses will continue to have some wealthy customers, for whom they can create extremely expensive clothes, but the bulk of their income will now come from mass sales.

Thus within the space of one hundred years haute couture has been stood on its head. Whereas it began as an exclusive art, which only the privileged could afford, by the middle of the twentieth century it was being forced to cater for wider tastes. Affluence was no longer the prerogative of the nobility, the buying power of the humble millions now called the tune, and Paris fashion houses had to bow before this new dictator. From being aristocratic haute couture had to become more democratic.

Notes

Chapter 1

1 D.J. de Marly, 'Fashionable Suppliers; leading tailors and clothing tradesmen in London 1660–1700', *Antiquaries Journal*, 58 ii, London, 1978.
2 D. Diderot and J. Le Rond d'Alembert, *Encyclopédie*, Paris, 1751–65.
3 P. de Nouvion and E. Liez, *Un Ministre des Modes sous Louis XVI: Mademoiselle Bertin, Marchande de Robes à la Reine, 1747–1813*, Henri Leclerc, Paris, 1911, p. 84.
4 H. Bouchot, *La Toilette à la Cour de Napoléon I*, Paris, 1895, pp. 6–7.
5 Baptismal Records, Abbey Church of SS Peter and Paul, Bourne, Lincolnshire.
6 J.P. Worth, *A Century of Fashion*, p. 5. This is the primary source for C.F. Worth's history, but it was published posthumously and contains errors of fact and date.
7 Great Exhibition of the Works of Industry of All Nations, Jury Reports, London, 1851, p. 1193.
8 Exposition Universelle, Paris, 1855, Liste Générale des Récompenses Décernées par le Jury International, p. 289.
9 Princess P. de Metternich, *Souvenirs 1859–1871*, pp. 135–45.
10 Mme Carette, *My Mistress, the Empress Eugénie; or, Court Life at the Tuileries*, p. 178.
11 C. Dickens, *All the Year Round*, vol. IX, 28 February 1863, p. 9.
12 C. Dickens, op. cit.
13 P. de Metternich, op. cit., pp. 142–4; E. and J. de Goncourt, *Journal*, vol. VI, entry for 9 September 1882; J.P. Worth, op. cit., p. 189.
14 H. Taine, *Notes sur Paris*, 1867, pp. 174–5.
15 P. de Metternich, op. cit., p. 140.

Chapter 2

1 J.C. Flügel, *The Psychology of Clothes*, Hogarth Press and the Institute of Psycho-Analysis, 1930, p. 138.
2 S. Pepys, *The Diary*, ed. R. Latham and W. Matthews, first complete edition, 1970 onwards, vol. II, entry for 3 December 1661.
3 F. Adolphus, *Some Memories of Paris*, p. 189.
4 R. König, *The Restless Image, a Sociology of Fashion*, trs. F. Bradley, George Allen and Unwin, 1973, p. 160.
5 R. König, ibid., p. 77.
6 F. Adolphus, op. cit., p. 190.
7 A. Adburgham, *A Punch History of Manners and Modes 1841–1940*, Hutchinson, 1961, p. 55.
8 H. Mayhew, *The Shops and Companies of London*, 1865, vol. 1, pp. 58–60.
9 Mme Carette, op. cit., pp. 173–5.
10 *Paris Fashion*, ed. R. Lynam, pp. 53 and 127.
11 J.P. Worth, op. cit., pp. 33–4.
12 A. Adburgham, op. cit., p. 135.
13 A. Adburgham, ibid., pp. 135–6.

Chapter 3

1 Consuelo Vanderbilt Balsan, *The Glitter and the Gold*, Harper & Bros., New York, 1952, pp. 68–9, and 33–4.
2 Paul Poiret, *En Habillant l'Epoque*, pp. 52–8.
3 F.H. Winterburn, *Principles of Correct Dress*. First two chapters by J.P. Worth, and last by Poiret; pp. 7–8 and 45–6.
4 Melba, *Melodies and Memories*, Thornton Butterworth, 1927, p. 151.
5 J.P. Worth, op. cit., p. 132.
6 P. Poiret, op. cit., pp. 53–4.
7 Jean D'Yvelet, *Le Journal*, 6 June 1910.
8 *The Standard*, 22 February 1913.
9 Cecil Beaton, *The Glass of Fashion*, pp. 120–7.
10 Marie Dormoy, *Jacques Doucet*, Abbéville, Paris, 1931, pp. 2–16.
11 Charles Creed, *Made to Measure*, pp. 12–17.

Chapter 4

1 D.J. de Marly, 'The Establishment of Roman Dress in Seventeenth-Century Portraiture', *Burlington Magazine*, no. 868, vol. CXVII, July 1975, pp. 443–51; and D.J. de Marly, 'Undress in the Oeuvre of Lely', *Burlington Magazine*, no. 908, vol. CXX, November 1978, pp. 749–50.
2 L.J. Beale, *The Laws of Health, in relation to the Mind and Body*, John Churchill, 1851, p. 46.
3 Mrs Merrifield, *Dress as a Fine Art*, pp. 103–6.
4 R.A. Caplin, *Health and Beauty; or, Corsets and Clothing constructed in accordance with the physiological laws of the Human Body*, Darton, 1856.
5 D.C. Bloomer, *The Life and Writings of Amelia Bloomer*, Arena, Boston, 1895, pp. 38–84.
6 W.M. Rossetti, *Pre-Raphaelite Diaries and Letters*, Hurst & Blackett, 1900, pp. 65–73.
7 W. Holman Hunt, *Pre-Raphaelitism and the Pre-Raphaelite Brotherhood*, Macmillan, 1905, vol. II, pp. 344–9.
8 S.M. Newton, *Health, Art and Reason*, John Murray, 1974, p. 34.
9 Luke Limner (pseudonym of J. Leighton), *Madre Natura versus The Moloch of Fashion*, Bradbury, Evans & Co., 1870.
10 M.S. Watts, *George Frederic Watts, The Annals of an Artist's Life*, vol. I, pp. 122–3.
11 Mrs Haweis, *The Art of Dress*, (no publisher given), 1879, p. 110 and chapter 10 *passim*.
12 Mrs J. Comyns Carr, *Reminiscences*, ed. Eve Adam, Hutchinson, 1925, pp. 79–80 and 85.
13 For du Maurier and the Aesthetic movement see L. Ormond, *George du Maurier*, Routledge and Kegan Paul, 1969, chapter 7.
14 W.P. Frith, *My Autobiography and Reminiscences*, Richard Bentley & Son, 1889, pp. 432–3.
15 A.S. Baillie, *The Science of Dress in Theory and Practice*, Sampson, Law, Marston, Searle & Rivington, 1885, pp. 182–8.
16 M.S. Watts, op. cit., vol. III, p. 203.
17 O. Wilde, *Pall Mall Gazette*, 14 October 1884, p. 6.
18 H. Tierlinck, *Henry van de Velde*, Monographies de l'Art Belge, Le Ministère de l'Instruction Publique, 1959, pp. 7–8.
19 J.P. Worth, op. cit., p. 53.

20 A. Adburgham, *Liberty's, A Biography of a Shop*, George Allen & Unwin, 1975, p. 63.
21 For the discomfort of late nineteenth century clothing see Gwen Raverat, *Period Piece*, Faber & Faber, 1952, pp. 253–67.

Chapter 5

1 Paul Poiret, op. cit., p. 63
2 Celia Bertin, *Paris à la Mode*, p. 168.
3 Lady Diana Cooper, *The Rainbow Comes and Goes*, Rupert Hart-Davis, 1958, p.60.
4 *Ottoline, the Early Memoirs of Lady Ottoline Morrell*, ed. Robert Gathorne-Hardy, pp. 168 and 276–7.
5 Palmer White, *Poiret*, Studio Vista, 1973.
6 Edna Woolman Chase and Ilka Chase, *Always in Vogue*, pp. 91–2.
7 Poiret, op. cit., pp. 142–55.
8 F.H. Winterburn, op. cit., p. 240.

Chapter 6

1 Diary of Count Primoli, trs. J.R. Richardson, *La Vie Parisienne 1852–1870*, Hamish Hamilton, 1971, pp. 240–1.
2 P. Poiret, op. cit., pp. 57–8.
3 E. Schiaparelli, *A Shocking Life*, p. 48.
4 E. & J. de Goncourt, op. cit., vol. VI, entry for 9 May 1879.
5 F.H. Winterburn, op. cit., p. 19.
6 F. Adolphus, op. cit., pp. 184–6.
7 P. Portrait, 'A Paris Model', R. Lynam (ed.), op. cit., p. 189.
8 *Complete Official Catalogue*, Paris Universal Exhibition 1867, 'Clothing for women', p. 412 and 'Crinolines', p. 399.
9 E.W. and I. Chase, op. cit., p. 43.
10 C. Dickens, op. cit., vol. X, 5 September 1863.
11 'Backstage at a Paris Fashion Show', *Picture Post*, 15 October 1938.

Chapter 7

1 P. Balmain, *My Years and Seasons*, p. 88.
2 R. Lynam ed., op. cit., p. 158.
3 Count Harry Kessler, *The Diaries of a Cosmopolitan 1918–1937*, trs. and ed. C. Kessler, Weidenfeld and Nicolson, 1971, p. 380.
4 R. Lynam, ed., op. cit., p. 175.
5 *Complete Official Catalogue*, Paris Universal Exhibition 1867, p. 412 and 399.
6 *Annuaire Statistique de la France*, vol. XX, 1900, Ministère de Commerce, p. 252; vol. XXXIII, 1913, Ministère du Travail et de la Prévoyance Sociale, p. 195.
7 'La France Industrielle', *L'Européen*, 28 May 1930.
8 E.W. and I. Chase, op. cit., pp. 94–7.

Chapter 8

1 N.W. Senior, *Conversations with M. Thiers, M. Guizot, and other distinguished persons during the Second Empire*, vol. II, pp. 114–5.
2 D. Cecil, *The Cecils of Hatfield House*, Constable, 1973, p. 252.
3 R. Gathorne-Hardy ed., op. cit., p.77.

4 E. Ewing, *History of Twentieth-Century Fashion*, Batsford, 1974, pp. 119–38.
5 N.W. Senior, op. cit., vol. II, p. 130.
6 R. Dudley Baxter, *The Taxation of the United Kingdom*, Macmillan, 1869, p. 14 and appendices II and III.
7 E.J. Hobsbawm, *Industry and Empire, an Economic History of Britain since 1750*, p. 130.
8 Mrs E. Pritchard, *The Cult of Chiffon*, Grant Richard, 1902, chapter VIII *passim*.
9 E.J. Hobsbawm, op. cit., pp. 137–40.

Chapter 9

1 M. Haedrich, *Coco Chanel Secrète*, Editions Robert Laffont, 1971; C. Baillen, *Chanel Solitaire*, trs. B. Bray, Collins, 1973.
2 E. Schiaparelli, op. cit., *passim*.
3 C. Bertin, op. cit., pp. 167–71.
4 C. Bertin, ibid.
5 C. Bertin, op. cit., p. 220; P. Portrait 'A Paris Model', R. Lynam (ed.), op. cit.
6 A. de Stoeckl, *My Dear Marquis*, John Murray, 1952, p. 208; R. Gimpel, *Diary of an Art Dealer*, trs. J. Rosenberg, Hodder and Stoughton, 1966, p. 137.
7 C. Bertin, op. cit., p. 185.
8 G. Lawrence, *A Star Danced*, W.H. Allen, 1945, p. 182; J. Ellis *The Duchess of Kent*, Odhams, 1952, p. 53.
9 D. McConathy, 'Mainbocher' in *American Fashion*, ed. S. Tomerlin Lee, Fashion Institute of Technology, André Deutsch, 1976, pp. 115–17.

Chapter 10

1 Lady Duff Gordon, *Discretions and Indiscretions*, Jarrolds, 1932.
2 H. Amies, *Just so Far*, p. 242.
3 Mrs C.S. Peel, *Life's Enchanted Cup*, John Lane at Bodley Head, 1933, p. 107; Loelia Grosvenor, Duchess of Westminster, *Grace and Favour*, Weidenfeld and Nicolson, 1961, p. 105.
4 N. Hartnell, *Silver and Gold*, Odhams, 1958; Z. Halls, *Coronation Costume 1685–1953*, catalogue of 1973 exhibition at the Museum of London, plate 24.
5 '40 Years of the IWS', special supplement of *Wool Record*, June 1977.
6 British *Vogue*, March 1946, p. 39.
7 H. Amies, op. cit., *passim*, and personal communication.
8 'London's Fashion Designers', British *Vogue*, February 1946, pp. 43–5.

Chapter 11

1 E.W. and I. Chase, op. cit., pp. 287 and 314–17.
2 P. Balmain, op. cit., pp. 62–78.
3 R. Lynam ed., op. cit., pp. 140–4.
4 P. Balmain, op. cit., pp. 88–117.
5 In May 1978 the Boussac empire was placed in the hands of the receivers when it was losing £1.2m. a month. Boussac had failed to see that cotton was being undermined by synthetic materials: *The Observer*, 4 June 1978.
6 R. Lynam ed., op. cit., pp. 169–77.
7 R. Lynam ed., op. cit., pp. 31–7, and 195–205.
8 For Mary Quant's own story see *Quant by Quant*, Cassell, 1966.

Bibliography

Adburgham, Alison, *A Punch History of Manners and Modes*, Hutchinson, 1961

Adolphus, F., *Some Memories of Paris*, Blackwood and Sons, 1895

Amies, Hardy, *Just so Far*, Collins, 1954

Balmain, Pierre, Trs. E. Lanchberry and G. Young, *My Years and Seasons*, Cassel, 1964

Beaton, Cecil, *The Glass of Fashion*, Weidenfeld and Nicolson, 1954

Bertin, Celia, Trs. M. Deans, *Paris à la Mode*, Gollancz, 1956

Carette, Mme, *My Mistress, the Empress Eugénie; or, Court Life at the Tuileries*, Dean and Son, 1889

Chase, Edna Woolman and Ilka, *Always in Vogue*, Gollancz, 1954

Creed, Charles, *Made to Measure*, Jarrolds, 1961

Dickens, Charles, *All the Year Round*, 1859–1870

Goncourt, Edmond and Jules de, *Journal*, Bibliothèque Charpentier, Paris, 1891

Hobsbawm, Eric, *Industry and Empire, an Economic History of Britain since 1750*, Weidenfeld and Nicolson, 1968

König, René, Trs. F. Bradley, *The Restless Image, a Sociology of Fashion*, Allen and Unwin, 1973

Lynam, Ruth, ed. *Paris Fashion*, Michael Joseph, 1972

Merrifield, Mary, *Dress as a Fine Art*, Arthur Hall, Virtue and Co., 1854

Metternich, Princess Pauline de, *Souvenirs 1859–1871*, Paris, 1922

Morrell, Lady Ottoline, ed. R. Gathorne-Hardy, *Ottoline, the Early Memoirs of Lady Ottoline Morrell*, Faber and Faber, 1963

Pepys, Samuel, *The Diary*, first complete transcription ed. R. Latham and W. Matthews, Bell and Sons, 1970

Poiret, Paul, *En Habillant l'Epoque*, Librairie Grasset, Paris, 1930

Schiaparelli, Elsa, *Shocking Life*, Dent and Sons, 1954

Senior, Nassau, ed. M.C.M. Simpson, *Conversations with M. Thiers, M. Guizot, and other distinguished persons during the Second Empire*, 1878

Watts, Mary, *George Frederic Watts, The Annals of an Artist's Life*, Macmillan, 1912

Winterburn, Florence, *Principles of Correct Dress*, Harper and Bros, New York, 1914

Worth, Jean-Philippe, Trs. Ruth Scott Miller, *A Century of Fashion*, Little, Brown and Co., Boston, 1928

Index